3rd Workshop on Continuous Vector Space Models and their Compositionality 2015

Co-located with ACL-IJCNLP 2015

Beijing, China
31 July 2015

ISBN: 978-1-5108-0942-0

Printed from e-media with permission by:

Curran Associates, Inc.
57 Morehouse Lane
Red Hook, NY 12571

proceedings.com

Some format issues inherent in the e-media version may also appear in this print version.

Printed by Curran Associates, Inc. (2015)

Association for Computational Linguistics
209 N. Eighth Street
Stroudsburg, Pennsylvania 18360

Phone: 1-570-476-8006
Fax: 1-570-476-0860

acl@aclweb.org

Additional copies of this publication are available from:

Curran Associates, Inc.
57 Morehouse Lane
Red Hook, NY 12571 USA
Phone: 845-758-0400
Fax: 845-758-2634
Email: curran@proceedings.com
Web: www.proceedings.com

ACL-IJCNLP 2015

The 3rd Workshop on Continuous Vector Space Models and their Compositionality (CVSC)

Proceedings of the Workshop

July 26-31, 2015
Beijing, China

Production and Manufacturing by
Taberg Media Group AB
Box 94, 562 02 Taberg
Sweden

Google™

Microsoft Research

Introduction

In most natural language processing applications the goal is to extract linguistic information from raw text or to transform linguistic observations into an alternative form, for instance from speech to text or one language to another. All of these applications often involve statistical models that rely heavily on a discrete representation of linguistic concepts, such as words and their POS tags, phrases and their syntactic categories or sentences, documents, etc. This includes any model parameterized with large probability tables or based on the extraction of multiple co-occurrence features (e.g. bigrams or tag/word pairs). Such a representation poorly models statistical structure not explicitly represented within the parameterization, but that might be very relevant from a morphological, syntactic and semantic standpoint. This hinders the generalization power of the model and reduces its ability to adapt to other domains. Another consequence is that such statistical models can only model very restricted contexts of text, without suffering from the sparsity of data. For instance, even the Google n-gram corpus only includes grams up to length 5. Data sparsity is a well-known and fundamental issue in statistical NLP, for which the existing remedies based on smoothing techniques can be insufficient.

In recent years, there has been a growing interest in algorithms that learn a continuous representation for words, phrases, or documents. For instance, one can see latent semantic analysis and latent Dirichlet allocation as a mapping of documents or words into a continuous lower dimensional topic-space. Another example, continuous word vector-space models, represent word meanings with vectors that capture semantic and syntactic information. These representations can be used to induce similarity measures by computing distances between the vectors, leading to many useful applications, such as information retrieval, search query expansions, document classification and question answering.

The idea of continuous vector spaces for language modeling has been used to develop neural language models that have reached state of the art performance in several applications. Another different trend of research on continuous vector space models belongs to the family of spectral methods developed to overcome some limitations of discrete latent space models. A further line of research is distributional semantic models that are historically more tied with linguistic theories.

Despite the success of single word vector space models, they are severely limited since they do not capture compositionality, the important quality of natural language that allows speakers to determine the meaning of a longer expression based on the meanings of its words and the rules used to combine them. This prevents them from gaining a deeper understanding of the semantics of longer phrases or sentences. For this reason, recently, there has been much progress in capturing compositionality in vector spaces.

Given this background, the first and second workshops on Continuous Vector Space Models and their Compositionality have been organized, and received high quality contributions, as well as high participation. As a result, this workshop has successfully served as a bridge between communities working on the different kinds of semantics models mentioned above. We believe, further progress on the applications of such models could be made by gathering both applied and theoretical researchers interested in developing systems that capture natural language semantics. This broader vision is reflected by the new list of topics this year. In addition, given the high interest and rapid development of various continuous semantic models, we invited more keynote speakers, compared to previous years.

This year, we continued in this direction, with the following list of topics:

- Neural networks
- Spectral methods
- Distributional semantic models

- Language modeling for automatic speech recognition, statistical machine translation, and information retrieval
- Automatic annotation of texts
- Unsupervised and semi-supervised word sense induction and disambiguation
- Phrase and sentence-level distributional representations
- The role of syntax in compositional models
- Formal and distributional semantic models
- Language modeling for logical and natural reasoning
- Integration of distributional representations with other models
- Multi-modal learning for distributional representations
- Knowledge base embedding

In brief, we aimed to highlight the ongoing effort to address some of these points, either by theoretical reasoning, or through example via demonstrating interesting properties of new or existing distributional models of semantics. We also aimed to gather formal semanticists, computational linguists, machine learning researchers and computational neuroscientists to tackle these fascinating problems.

Organizers:

Alexandre Allauzen, LIMSI-CNRS/Université Paris-Sud
Edward Grefenstette, Google DeepMind
Karl Moritz Hermann, Google DeepMind
Hugo Larochelle, Université de Sherbrooke
Scott Wen-tau Yih, Microsoft Research

Organizers:

Alexandre Allauzen, LIMSI-CNRS/Université Paris-Sud
Edward Grefenstette, Google DeepMind
Karl Moritz Hermann, Google DeepMind
Hugo Larochelle, Université de Sherbrooke
Scott Wen-tau Yih, Microsoft Research

Program Committee:

Marco Baroni, University of Trento
Yoshua Bengio, Université de Montreal
Phil Blunsom, University of Oxford
Antoine Bordes, Facebook
Leon Bottou, Microsoft
Stephen Clark, University of Cambridge
Shay Cohen, University of Edinburgh
Georgiana Dinu, University of Trento
Kevin Duh, Nara Institute of Science and Technology
Andriy Mnih, Google DeepMind
Mehrnoosh Sadrzadeh, University of London
Mark Steedman, University of Edinburgh
Peter Turney, NRC
Jason Weston, Facebook
Guillaume Wisniewski, LIMSI-CNRS

Invited Speaker:

Kyunghyun Cho, Université de Montréal
Stephen Clark, University of Cambridge
Yoav Goldberg, Bar Ilan University
Ray Mooney, University of Texas at Austin
Percy Liang, Stanford University

Table of Contents

Conference Program

Friday, July 31, 2015

09:00–09:05 ***Opening Remarks***

09:05–09:50 ***INVITED TALK - Kyunghyun Cho***

09:50–10:10 ***CONTRIBUTED TALK - Observed versus latent features for knowledge base and text inference, Kristina Toutanova and Danqi Chen***

10:10–10:30 ***CONTRIBUTED TALK - Learning Embeddings for Transitive Verb Disambiguation by Implicit Tensor Factorization, Kazuma Hashimoto and Yoshimasa Tsuruoka***

10:30–11:00 ***Coffee Break***

11:00–11:45 ***INVITED TALK - Yoav Goldberg***

11:45–12:30 ***INVITED TALK - Percy Liang***

12:30–14:00 ***Lunch***

14:00–14:45 ***INVITED TALK - Stephen Clark***

14:45–15:30 ***INVITED TALK - Ray Mooney***

15:30–16:00 ***Coffee Break***

16:00–17:00 ***Poster session***

Learning Embeddings for Transitive Verb Disambiguation by Implicit Tensor Factorization
Kazuma Hashimoto and Yoshimasa Tsuruoka

Recursive Neural Networks Can Learn Logical Semantics
Samuel R. Bowman, Christopher Potts and Christopher D. Manning

Concept Extensions as the Basis for Vector-Space Semantics: Combining Distributional and Ontological Information about Entities
Jackie Chi Kit Cheung

Joint Semantic Relevance Learning with Text Data and Graph Knowledge
Dongxu Zhang, Bin Yuan, Dong Wang and Rong Liu

Exploring the effect of semantic similarity for Phrase-based Machine Translation
Kunal Sachdeva and Dipti Sharma

Incremental Adaptation Strategies for Neural Network Language Models
Alex Ter-Sarkisov, Holger Schwenk, Fethi Bougares and Loïc Barrault

Observed versus latent features for knowledge base and text inference
Kristina Toutanova and Danqi Chen

17:00–17:30 ***Panel***

Learning Embeddings for Transitive Verb Disambiguation by Implicit Tensor Factorization

Kazuma Hashimoto and Yoshimasa Tsuruoka
The University of Tokyo, 3-7-1 Hongo, Bunkyo-ku, Tokyo, Japan
{hassy,tsuruoka}@logos.t.u-tokyo.ac.jp

Abstract

We present an implicit tensor factorization method for learning the embeddings of transitive verb phrases. Unlike the implicit matrix factorization methods recently proposed for learning word embeddings, our method directly models the interaction between predicates and their two arguments, and learns verb phrase embeddings. By representing transitive verbs as matrices, our method captures multiple meanings of transitive verbs and disambiguates them taking their arguments into account. We evaluate our method on a widely-used verb disambiguation task and three phrase similarity tasks. On the disambiguation task, our method outperforms previous state-of-the-art methods. Our experimental results also show that adjuncts provide useful information in learning the meanings of verb phrases.

1 Introduction

There is a growing interest in learning vector-space representations of words and phrases using large training corpora in the field of Natural Language Processing (NLP) (Mikolov et al., 2013; Mitchell and Lapata, 2010). The phrase representations are usually computed by composition models that combine the meanings of words into the meanings of phrases. While some studies focus on representing entire phrases or sentences using syntactic structures (Hermann and Blunsom, 2013; Socher et al., 2011), others focus on representing the meaning of transitive verb phrases (Grefenstette and Sadrzadeh, 2011; Grefenstette et al., 2013; Kartsaklis et al., 2012).

In this paper, we investigate vector-space representations of transitive verb phrases. The meaning of a transitive verb is often ambiguous and disambiguated by its arguments, i.e., subjects and objects. Investigation of transitive verb phrases should therefore provide insights into how composition models can capture such semantic interactions between words. Moreover, in practice, capturing the meanings of transitive verb phrases should be useful in many real-world NLP applications such as semantic retrieval (Miyao et al., 2006) and question answering (*Who did What to Whom?*) (Srihari and Li, 2000).

There are several approaches to representing transitive verb phrases in a vector space using large unannotated corpora. One is based on tensor calculus (Grefenstette and Sadrzadeh, 2011; Kartsaklis et al., 2012; Van de Cruys et al., 2013) and another is based on neural networks (Hashimoto et al., 2014; Muraoka et al., 2014; Tsubaki et al., 2013). In the tensor-based methods, transitive verbs are represented as matrices, and they are constructed by using the pre-trained word embeddings of their subjects and objects. One limitation of this approach is that the embeddings of subject-verb-object phrases are computed statically, i.e., the composition process and the embedding (or matrix) construction process are conducted separately. In the neural network-based methods, the embeddings of words and phrases can be learned jointly (Hashimoto et al., 2014). However, the strong interaction between verbs and their arguments is not fully captured in their method because it relies on shallow neural networks using diagonal weight matrices which are designed to work on large training corpora.

To bridge the gap between the two approaches, we present an implicit tensor factorization method

Proceedings of the 3rd Workshop on Continuous Vector Space Models and their Compositionality (CVSC), pages 1–11,
Beijing, China, July 26-31, 2015.

for learning the embeddings of transitive verb phrases. We assume a three-mode tensor in which the value of each element represents the level of plausibility of a tuple of a predicate and its two arguments (Van de Cruys et al., 2013). We then implicitly factorize the tensor into three latent factors, namely one predicate tensor and two argument matrices. This is motivated by the recently proposed implicit matrix factorization methods for learning word embeddings (Levy and Goldberg, 2014; Mikolov et al., 2013). Our method trains matrices representing predicates and embeddings of their arguments so that they maximize the accuracy of predicting the plausibility of the predicate-argument tuples in the training corpus. The transitive verb matrices and the embeddings of their subject and object are thus jointly learned. Furthermore, this method allows us to exploit the role of prepositional adjuncts when learning the meaning of verb phrases by modeling the relationship between prepositions and verb phrases.

Our experimental results show that our method enables predicates and their arguments to strongly interact with each other and that adjuncts are useful in learning the meaning of verb phrases. We evaluate our method using a widely-used verb disambiguation task and three phrase similarity tasks. On the disambiguation dataset provided by Grefenstette and Sadrzadeh (2011), we have achieved a Spearman's rank correlation score of 0.614, which is significantly higher than the state of the art (0.456). This result demonstrates that the direct interaction between verbs and their arguments is important in tackling verb disambiguation tasks. Qualitative evaluation further shows that the meanings of ambiguous verbs can be disambiguated according to their arguments and the learned verb matrices capture multiple meanings of transitive verbs.

2 Method

To learn the embeddings of transitive verb phrases, we focus on the role of adjuncts, which optionally complement the meaning of the verb phrases. For example, in the following sentence, the prepositional phrase starting from the preposition "in" is an adjunct of the verb "make":

> An importer might be able to make payment in his own domestic currency.

The transitive verb "make" is inherently ambiguous, but this sentence tells us that the action expressed by the verb phrase "make payment" is carried out by means of a currency. If we further observe the verb phrase "pay money" with a similar adjunct in another sentence, those two sentences tell us that the two phrases "make payment" and "pay money" are semantically similar to each other. We therefore expect such prepositional adjuncts to be useful in learning the meaning of verb phrases. In the disambiguation processes, strong interactions between transitive verbs and their arguments are desirable as with the method in Tsubaki et al. (2013). More specifically, the meaning of "make" changes according to its object "payment" and the meaning of "pay" changes according to its object "money".

Predicate	Argument 1	Argument 2
make	an importer	payment
in	make payment	his own domestic currency

Table 1: Example output from the Enju parser.

Predicate	Argument 1	Argument 2
make	importer	payment
in	importer make payment	currency

Table 2: Modified examples.

We use the probabilistic HPSG parser *Enju*[1] (Miyao and Tsujii, 2008) to identify transitive verbs with their subjects and objects, and as adjuncts, we also extract prepositional phrases with transitive verbs. In the grammar of the Enju parser, each word in a sentence is a predicate with zero or more arguments, i.e., prepositions, too, are treated as predicates.

In the example sentence shown above, the transitive verb "make" and the preposition "in" are predicates which take two arguments. Table 1 shows the output from the Enju parser. In this example, the transitive verb "make" takes two arguments: the first argument (the subject) is the noun phrase "an importer" and the second argument (the object) is the noun "payment". The preposition "in" also takes two arguments: the first argument is the verb phrase "make payment" and the second argument is the noun phrase "his own domestic currency". For simplicity we use only the head word of each noun phrase, so the subjects and objects of the transitive verbs are nouns and the second arguments of the prepositions are also nouns. We further modify the output by incorporating the

[1] http://kmcs.nii.ac.jp/enju/.

subject for each verb phrase which is the first argument of prepositions when the subject exists [2]. Therefore, the words used in this paper are verbs, nouns, and prepositions. Table 2 shows the modified output of the examples in Table 1.

To model the co-occurrence statistics of predicate-argument structures, we follow Van de Cruys et al. (2013) and assume a three-mode tensor, which is just a three-dimensional array, $\mathcal{T} \in \mathbb{R}^{|\mathbb{P}|\times|\mathbb{A}_1|\times|\mathbb{A}_2|}$ in which plausibility scores are stored as real values. $\mathbb{P}$ is the set of predicates of a particular category in the training corpus, $\mathbb{A}_1$ is the set of the first argument of the predicates in $\mathbb{P}$, and $\mathbb{A}_2$ is the set of the second argument. When treating transitive verbs as predicates, $\mathbb{A}_1$ is the set of their subjects and $\mathbb{A}_2$ is the set of their objects. Table 1 shows an example, where "make", "an importer", and "payment" are a member of $\mathbb{P}$, $\mathbb{A}_1$, and $\mathbb{A}_2$, respectively. The plausibility score $\mathcal{T}(i, j, k)$ corresponds to the tuple of the i-th ($1 \leq i \leq |\mathbb{P}|$) predicate having the j-th ($1 \leq j \leq |\mathbb{A}_1|$) first-argument and the k-th ($1 \leq k \leq |\mathbb{A}_2|$) second-argument. The larger the value of $\mathcal{T}(i, j, k)$ is, the more plausible the tuple (i, j, k) is. In the above example, if the tuple (i, j, k) corresponds to "make", "an importer", and "payment" and i' corresponds to "eat", the value of $\mathcal{T}(i, j, k)$ is expected to be larger than that of $\mathcal{T}(i', j, k)$.

As with Van de Cruys et al. (2013), we factorize the large three-mode tensor $\mathcal{T}$ into three factors:

- three-mode tensor $\mathcal{P} \in \mathbb{R}^{|\mathbb{P}|\times d\times d}$,
- matrix $\mathbf{A}_1 \in \mathbb{R}^{d\times|\mathbb{A}_1|}$, and
- matrix $\mathbf{A}_2 \in \mathbb{R}^{d\times|\mathbb{A}_2|}$.

The dimensionality d is a hyperparameter that determines the size of the latent factors. Using these factors, we can compute a plausibility score:

$$\mathcal{T}(i, j, k) = \mathbf{a}_1(j)^{\mathrm{T}}\mathbf{P}(i)\mathbf{a}_2(k) \qquad (1)$$

where $\mathbf{a}_1(j) \in \mathbb{R}^{d\times 1}$ and $\mathbf{a}_2(k) \in \mathbb{R}^{d\times 1}$ are the j-th and k-th column vectors of $\mathbf{A}_1$ and $\mathbf{A}_2$, respectively, and $\mathbf{P}(i) \in \mathbb{R}^{d\times d}$ is the i-th slice, which is just a matrix, of $\mathcal{P}$. $\mathbf{a}_1(j)^{\mathrm{T}}$ is the transpose of $\mathbf{a}_1(j)$. By this tensor factorization, each predicate in $\mathbb{P}$ is represented with a matrix, which we call a predicate matrix, and each argument in $\mathbb{A}_1$ and $\mathbb{A}_2$ is represented with a vector, which we call an argument embedding. As with Hashimoto et al. (2014), arguments are not restricted to words in our method, and thus we compute argument embeddings using a composition function when the arguments consist of more than two words.

To learn the predicate matrices and argument embeddings, we define a plausibility judgment task by using a cost function for each predicate-argument tuple observed in the training corpus. For each predicate-argument tuple (i, j, k), the cost function $E(i, j, k)$ is defined as follows:

$$\begin{aligned} -\log\sigma(\mathcal{T}(i,j,k)) &- \log(1-\sigma(\mathcal{T}(i',j,k))) \\ &- \log(1-\sigma(\mathcal{T}(i,j',k))) \\ &- \log(1-\sigma(\mathcal{T}(i,j,k'))) \end{aligned} \qquad (2)$$

where $i' \in \mathbb{P}$ is a randomly drawn predicate, and $j' \in \mathbb{A}_1$ and $k' \in \mathbb{A}_2$ are randomly drawn arguments. $\sigma(x)$ is the logistic function, so the cost function $E(i, j, k)$ in Eq. (2) measures whether we can discriminate between the plausible tuple and other three implausible tuples by means of logistic regressions. We follow Mikolov et al. (2013) to draw the random predicates and arguments according to their frequencies weighted by an exponent of 0.75 and ensure that each of the randomly generated tuples is not observed in the corpus. The overall objective function is defined as the sum of the cost functions for all observed predicate-argument tuples and minimized by AdaGrad (Duchi et al., 2011) in a mini-batch setting.

The partial derivative $\frac{\partial E(i,j,k)}{\partial \mathbf{P}(i)}$ for updating the model parameters is computed as follows:

$$\begin{aligned} \frac{\partial E(i,j,k)}{\partial \mathbf{P}(i)} = (\sigma(\mathcal{T}(i,j,k)) - 1)&\mathbf{a}_1(j) \otimes \mathbf{a}_2(k) + \\ \sigma(\mathcal{T}(i,j',k))&\mathbf{a}_1(j') \otimes \mathbf{a}_2(k) + \\ \sigma(\mathcal{T}(i,j,k'))&\mathbf{a}_1(j) \otimes \mathbf{a}_2(k') \end{aligned} \qquad (3)$$

where $\otimes$ denotes the outer-product of two vectors. Similarly, the partial derivatives $\frac{\partial E(i,j,k)}{\partial \mathbf{a}_1(j)}$ and $\frac{\partial E(i,j,k)}{\partial \mathbf{a}_2(k)}$ are computed as follows:

$$\begin{aligned} \frac{\partial E(i,j,k)}{\partial \mathbf{a}_1(j)} = (\sigma(\mathcal{T}(i,j,k)) - 1)&\mathbf{P}(i)\mathbf{a}_2(k) + \\ \sigma(\mathcal{T}(i',j,k))&\mathbf{P}(i')\mathbf{a}_2(k) + \\ \sigma(\mathcal{T}(i,j,k'))&\mathbf{P}(i)\mathbf{a}_2(k') \end{aligned} \qquad (4)$$

[2] Subjects can be absent. For example, in the sentence "Learning word embedings is interesting" the subject of the transitive verb "learn" is absent.

$$\frac{\partial E(i,j,k)}{\partial \mathbf{a}_2(k)} = (\sigma(\mathcal{T}(i,j,k)) - 1)\mathbf{P}(i)^{\mathrm{T}}\mathbf{a}_1(j) + \sigma(\mathcal{T}(i',j,k))\mathbf{P}(i')^{\mathrm{T}}\mathbf{a}_1(j) + \sigma(\mathcal{T}(i,j',k))\mathbf{P}(i)^{\mathrm{T}}\mathbf{a}_1(j') \quad (5)$$

which can be used to learn the composition function using the backpropagation algorithm if the arguments are not words. When the arguments are words, we then use the partial derivatives to directly update the argument embeddings. $\mathbf{P}(i')$, $\mathbf{a}_1(j')$, and $\mathbf{a}_2(k')$ are also updated but for the sake of brevity the partial derivatives for them are not shown here. Equation (3) shows that a predicate matrix is updated to capture the information about which argument pairs are or are not relevant to the predicate. Argument embeddings are learned to capture similar information.

2.1 Transitive Verb Phrases with Adjuncts

While our method is applicable to any categories of predicates which take two arguments, in this paper, we focus on learning the embeddings of transitive verb phrases by treating transitive verbs and prepositions as predicates. Thus, we factorize two tensors $\mathcal{T}_v$ and $\mathcal{T}_p$ for transitive verbs and prepositions, respectively. $\mathcal{T}_v$ is factorized into a verb tensor $\mathcal{V}$ (corresponding to $\mathcal{P}$), a subject matrix $\mathbf{S}$ (corresponding to $\mathbf{A}_1$), and an object matrix $\mathbf{O}$ (corresponding to $\mathbf{A}_2$). To compute argument embeddings composed by subject-verb-object tuples, we use the *copy-subject* function in Kartsaklis et al. (2012):

$$\mathbf{s}(m) \odot (\mathbf{V}(l)\mathbf{o}(n)) \quad (6)$$

where $\mathbf{V}(l)$ is a verb matrix, $\mathbf{s}(m)$ is a subject embedding, and $\mathbf{o}(n)$ is an object embedding. $\odot$ denotes the element-wise multiplication of two vectors. The composed verb phrase embeddings are taken as the first arguments of the prepositions. The copy-subject function is also used to compute verb-object phrase embeddings by omitting the subject embedding in Eq. (6):

$$\mathbf{V}(l)\mathbf{o}(n) \quad (7)$$

Compared with other composition functions defined in Kartsaklis et al. (2012), such as the copy-object function, the copy-subject function allows us to compute embeddings for both of subject-verb-object and verb-object phrases.

In the case of the copy-subject function, assuming that Eq. (4) is defined as $\boldsymbol{\delta}_1$, the subject embedding in Eq. (6) is updated using the following partial derivative:

$$\frac{\partial E(i,j,k)}{\partial \mathbf{s}(m)} = \boldsymbol{\delta}_1 \odot (\mathbf{V}(l)\mathbf{o}(n)) \quad (8)$$

We then define $\boldsymbol{\delta}_2$ as follows:

$$\boldsymbol{\delta}_2 = \boldsymbol{\delta}_1 \odot \mathbf{s}(m) \quad (9)$$

and update the verb matrix and object embedding using $\boldsymbol{\delta}_2$:

$$\frac{\partial E(i,j,k)}{\partial \mathbf{V}(l)} = \boldsymbol{\delta}_2 \mathbf{o}(n)^{\mathrm{T}} \quad (10)$$

$$\frac{\partial E(i,j,k)}{\partial \mathbf{o}(n)} = \mathbf{V}(l)^{\mathrm{T}} \boldsymbol{\delta}_2 \quad (11)$$

The model parameters used in the composition function are shared across the overall proposed method. That is, the verb matrices and subject/object embeddings are used for computing the composed embeddings and the plausibility scores in Eq. (1).

2.2 Relationship to Previous Work

Representing transitive verbs with matrices and computing transitive verb phrase embeddings have been proposed by Grefenstette and Sadrzadeh (2011) and others (Kartsaklis et al., 2012; Milajevs et al., 2014; Polajnar et al., 2014). All of them first construct word embeddings by using existing methods and then compute or learn transitive verb matrices. This kind of approach requires one to figure out which word embeddings are suitable for each method or task (Milajevs et al., 2014). By contrast, our method does not require any other word embedding methods and instead jointly learns word embeddings and matrices from scratch, which saves us from the time-consuming process to test which word representations learned by existing methods are suitable for which composition models. Moreover, our method *learns* the embeddings of transitive verb phrases by using adjuncts rather than statically computing them using learned word embeddings and matrices as done in the previous work.

The information stored in the verb matrices learned by Eq. (3) is similar to that in Grefenstette and Sadrzadeh (2011). In Grefenstette and Sadrzadeh (2011), a verb matrix is computed by the sum of the outer-products of the embeddings of its subject-object pairs observed in the corpus. By using such matrices, Kartsaklis et al. (2012) proposed the copy-subject function which has proven effective in representing transitive verb phrases. Using the copy-subject function is therefore a reasonable choice for our composition function.

The use of adjuncts constructed by prepositional phrases for learning verb phrase embeddings has been presented in Hashimoto et al. (2014). However, they used a variety of categories of predicates simultaneously, and thus it is not clear how adjuncts are useful in improving the embeddings of transitive verb phrases. In this paper, we use only transitive verbs and prepositions and clarify the effects of adjuncts. Moreover, the interactions between predicates and their arguments are weak in their method because their method relies on shallow neural networks using diagonal weight matrices. In contrast, our method allows the predicates to directly interact with their arguments.

The way of factorizing the three-mode tensors is based on Van de Cruys et al. (2013). The main difference between our method and theirs is that our method can treat phrases as the arguments. Their method is based on co-occurrence count statistics, and thus it is not straightforward to modify their method to treat phrases as well as words.

Our implicit tensor factorization method is motivated by Levy and Goldberg (2014). They introduced a way to interpret the recently developed word embedding learning method (Mikolov et al., 2013) by using matrix factorization. While their method only produces embeddings of single tokens, our method jointly learns word and phrase embeddings by focusing on the relationship between predicates and their two arguments.

3 Experimental Settings

3.1 Training Corpora

We separately used two corpora as our training corpora. The first one is the British National Corpus (BNC), from which we extracted 6 million sentences. The second one is a snapshot of the English Wikipedia[3] (enWiki) from November 2013. We extracted 80 million sentences from the original Wikipedia file. We then used the Enju parser (Miyao and Tsujii, 2008) to parse all the extracted sentences.

[3]http://dumps.wikimedia.org/enwiki/

Using the parsing results, we constructed the vocabulary for each training corpus. To be more specific, we used the 100,000 most frequent base-form words paired with their corresponding part-of-speech tags in each corpus. Using verbs, nouns, and prepositions in the vocabulary, we extracted predicate-argument tuples whose predicate categories are *verb_arg12* or *prep_arg12* defined in the Enju parser. We then pre-processed the output as shown in Table 2. Consequently, BNC consists of about 1.38 million instances (1.23 million types) for the verb data and about 0.93 million instances (0.88 million types) for the preposition data, and enWiki consists of about 23.6 million instances (15.8 million types) for the verb data and about 17.3 million instances (13.5 million types) for the preposition data. We call the verb data **SVO** and the combination of the two data **SVOPN**[4].

For each corpus, we randomly split the data into the training data (80%), the development data (10%), and the test data (10%). We used the development data for tuning hyperparameters to be used in downstream NLP tasks. When splitting the data, we ensured that each type of predicate-argument tuples appeared in only one of the three parts. Hence, for example, instances in the test data do not appear in either of the training or the development data.

To evaluate our method on the plausibility judgment task, for each predicate-argument tuple type in the development and the test data, we randomly sampled implausible tuples N times in the same way as defining the cost function in Eq. (2). That is, we prepared N sets of the development and the test data. For each set of the development and the test data, we calculated the accuracy of the plausibility judgment task; concretely, for each type of predicate-argument tuples (i, j, k), we evaluated whether $\mathcal{T}(i, j, k)$ is larger than all of $\mathcal{T}(i', j, k)$, $\mathcal{T}(i, j', k)$, and $\mathcal{T}(i, j, k')$ and then calculated the ratio of the number of types counted as correct to the total number of the types in the development or the test data. Finally, we calculated the average accuracy of the N set. For BNC, we set N to 50 and for enWiki we set N to 10.

[4]The training data, the training code, and the learned model parameters used in this paper are publicly available at http://www.logos.t.u-tokyo.ac.jp/~hassy/publications/cvsc2015/

3.2 Initialization and Hyperparameters

We initialized the noun embeddings, the verb matrices, and the preposition matrices with zero-mean gaussian noise with a variance of $\frac{1}{d}$, $\frac{1}{d^2}$, and $\frac{1}{d^2}$, respectively. The hyperparameters for training the embeddings and the matrices are the embedding dimensionality d, the learning rate α for AdaGrad (Duchi et al., 2011), the mini-batch size, and the number of iterations n over the training data. In our preliminary experiments, we have found that varying the mini-batch size is not so influential in our experimental results. We thus fixed the mini-batch size to 100. For other hyperparameters, we set d to $\{25, 50, 100\}$, α to $\{0.01, 0.02, 0.04, 0.06, 0.08, 0.1\}$, and the maximum number of n to 20. We selected the values of the hyperparameters so that the accuracy of the plausibility task was maximized on the development data described in Section 3.1.

3.3 Baseline Method

We mainly compared our method with the method called *PAS-CLBLM* in Hashimoto et al. (2014) since PAS-CLBLM is designed to learn composed representations as well as word embeddings using a variety of predicate-argument structures. PAS-CLBLM is modeled as a word predication model using predicate-argument structures, which means that, as with our method, the training relies on the co-occurrence statistics of predicate-argument structures. PAS-CLBLM achieved state-of-the-art results on transitive verb phrase similarity tasks. To train PAS-CLBLM, we used the same data described in Section 3.1. We selected the Wadd_{nl} function in PAS-CLBLM to compute the embedding of each subject-verb-object tuple (i, j, k):

$$\tanh(\mathbf{w}_\text{s} \odot \mathbf{s}(j) + \mathbf{w}_\text{v} \odot \mathbf{v}(i) + \mathbf{w}_\text{o} \odot \mathbf{o}(k)) \quad (12)$$

where $\mathbf{w}_\text{s}, \mathbf{w}_\text{v}, \mathbf{w}_\text{o} \in \mathbb{R}^{d \times 1}$ are the weight vectors (or the diagonal weight matrices) for composition and $\mathbf{s}(j), \mathbf{v}(i), \mathbf{o}(k) \in \mathbb{R}^{d \times 1}$ are the embeddings of the subjects, verbs, and objects, respectively. PAS-CLBLM has the same hyperparameters as our method described in Section 3.2. We used the development data for tuning the hyperparameters and added $d = 200$ to the candidate values for d since PAS-CLBLM is computationally less expensive than our method. We thus evaluated PAS-CLBLM also on the plausibility judgment task. Concretely, for each type of predicate-argument tuples (i, j, k) in the development data, the tuple is counted as correct when the predication scores for i, j, and k are larger than those for i', j', and k', respectively.

	d	BNC Acc. (%)	enWiki Acc. (%)
Our method	25	57.44 (0.11)	64.77 (0.03)
	50	**57.80** (0.11)	66.98 (0.03)
	100	57.48 (0.10)	**68.18** (0.03)
PAS-CLBLM	25	54.44 (0.14)	60.40 (0.03)
	50	**55.69** (0.13)	63.42 (0.02)
	100	55.66 (0.12)	64.81 (0.02)
	200	55.48 (0.15)	**65.20** (0.03)

Table 3: Evaluation results on the plausibility judgment task on the SVO development data.

4 Results and Discussion

We first tuned the hyperparameters in both our method and the baseline method using the plausibility judgment task. Table 3 shows the average accuracy with the standard deviation for each dimensionality on the SVO development data[5]. As shown in the table, our method outperforms PAS-CLBLM on both BNC and enWiki. The number of the model parameters in PAS-CLBLM ($d = 200$) is larger than that of the model parameters in our method ($d = 50$). This result demonstrates that the model architecture itself is more important than the number of the model parameters. The results on the SVO test data were 57.76% (our method, $d = 50$) and 55.66% (PAS-CLBLM, $d = 50$) for BNC. For enWiki, the results were 68.18% (our method, $d = 100$) and 65.19% (PAS-CLBLM, $d = 200$). We observed a similar trend on the SVOPN data and in the next section, for each embedding dimensionality, we used the model parameters which performed best on the plausibility task.

4.1 Evaluation on Transitive Verb Tasks

4.1.1 Evaluation Settings

We evaluated the learned embeddings of transitive verbs using a transitive verb disambiguation task and three tasks for measuring the semantic similarity between transitive verb phrases. Each phrase

[5]Van de Cruys (2014) reported much higher accuracy in a similar evaluation setting with a neural network model, but as discussed in Chambers and Jurafsky (2010), this is because using the uniform distribution over words for producing implausible tuples leads to optimistic results.

[6]We replicated the results reported in their paper using the model parameters publicly provided at `http://www.logos.t.u-tokyo.ac.jp/~hassy/publications/emnlp2014/`.

	Data	d	Dis. GS'11	Phrase similarity ML'10	KS'13	KS'14
Our method	SVO	25	0.410	0.511	0.392	0.440
		50	0.374	0.550	0.164	0.290
		100	0.373	0.474	0.312	0.418
	SVOPN	25	**0.574**	0.543	0.439	0.432
		50	0.535	**0.586**	0.403	0.397
		100	0.508	0.545	**0.487**	**0.517**
PAS-CLBLM	SVO	25	0.270	0.601	0.592	0.722
		50	**0.412**	0.581	0.523	0.721
		100	0.390	0.463	0.465	0.699
		200	0.369	0.458	0.434	0.602
	SVOPN	25	0.241	0.562	0.550	0.715
		50	0.281	**0.605**	**0.590**	**0.760**
		100	0.337	0.593	0.585	0.758
		200	0.342	0.561	0.549	0.744
Milajevs et al. (2014)			0.456	n/a	n/a	0.732
Hashimoto et al. (2014)[6]			0.422	0.669	0.612	0.770
Polajnar et al. (2014)			0.35	n/a	0.58	n/a

Table 4: Results for the transitive verb tasks using the BNC data.

	Data	d	Dis. GS'11	Phrase similarity ML'10	KS'13	KS'14
Our method	SVO	25	0.438	0.403	0.255	0.406
		50	0.480	0.416	0.359	0.481
		100	0.433	0.392	0.239	0.409
	SVOPN	25	0.576	0.435	0.372	0.555
		50	**0.614**	0.495	**0.422**	**0.566**
		100	0.576	**0.558**	0.420	0.548
PAS-CLBLM	SVO	25	0.342	0.500	0.407	0.624
		50	0.313	0.527	0.502	0.710
		100	0.358	0.534	0.470	0.655
		200	0.361	0.535	0.459	0.653
	SVOPN	25	0.171	0.571	**0.583**	0.697
		50	0.320	0.501	0.518	0.729
		100	0.321	**0.606**	0.540	0.742
		200	**0.374**	0.588	0.515	**0.744**
Milajevs et al. (2014)			0.456	n/a	n/a	0.732
Hashimoto et al. (2014)			0.422	0.669	0.612	0.770
Polajnar et al. (2014)			0.35	n/a	0.58	n/a

Table 5: Results for the transitive verb tasks using the enWiki data.

pair in the four datasets is paired with multiple human ratings: the higher the rating is, the more semantically similar the phrases are. To evaluate the learned verb phrase embeddings on each dataset, we used the Spearman's rank correlation between the human ratings and the cosine similarity between the phrase embeddings. We calculated the correlation scores using averaged human ratings. Each phrase pair in the datasets was annotated by more than two annotators and we took the average of the multiple human ratings for each phrase pair.

Transitive verb disambiguation. The first dataset **GS'11** is provided by Grefenstette and Sadrzadeh (2011). GS'11 consists of pairs of transitive verbs and each verb pair takes the same subject and object. As discussed in previous work (Kartsaklis and Sadrzadeh, 2013; Milajevs et al., 2014; Polajnar et al., 2014), GS'11 has an aspect of a verb sense disambiguation task. For example, the transitive verb "run" is known as a polysemous word and this task requires one to identify the meanings of "run" and "operate" are similar to each other when taking "people" as their subject and "company" as their object. In the same setting, however, the meanings of "run" and "move" are not similar to each other. The task is suitable for evaluating our method since our method allows verbs and their subjects and objects to multiplicatively interact with each other.

Transitive verb phrase similarity. The other datasets are **ML'10** provided by Mitchell and Lapata (2010), **KS'13** provided by Kartsaklis and Sadrzadeh (2013), and **KS'14** provided by Kartsaklis and Sadrzadeh (2014). ML'10 consists of pairs of verb-object phrases and KS'13 complements ML'10 by incorporating an appropriate subject for each verb-object phrase. KS'14 is the re-annotated version of KS'13 using a cloud sourcing service. Unlike GS'11, these three datasets require one to capture the topical similarity rather than the disambiguation aspect (Polajnar et al., 2014).

4.1.2 Result Overview

Table 4 and 5 show the evaluation results using BNC and enWiki, respectively. The results are shown for each method, data type, and embedding dimensionality. These tables also show the results from other work (Hashimoto et al., 2014; Milajevs et al., 2014; Polajnar et al., 2014) on the same tasks while the training settings, such as the corpus and information used in the training, are different from those in this work. However, the evaluation settings are the same with those in the previous work. That is, in the previous work, averaged human ratings were used to evaluate the Spearman's rank correlation scores, similarity scores between subject-verb-object phrases were used for GS'11, KS'13, and KS'14, and similarity scores between verb-object phrases were used for ML'10.

Effects of using adjuncts. Except for the results for GS'11 using PAS-CLBLM, the correla-

	Our method				PAS-CLBLM	
	SVO		SVOPN		SVOPN	
	make dollar	make saving	make cash	earn billion	make cash	make penny
make	make pay	use money	make dollar	earn million	make dollar	make baht
money	make profit	make cent	make profit	make gamble	make yen	make salary
	make cash	do business	earn baht	make pound	make pay	make profit
	earn profit	sell coin	earn pound	earn earning	make fund	make rupee
	make repayment	make expenditure	make loan	pay reimbursement	make loan	make cost
make	make loan	pay subsidy	make repayment	pay remuneration	make repayment	make receipt
payment	pay amount	pay deposit	pay fine	make raise	make compensation	make guarantee
	make offer	make transaction	pay amount	pay cost	make expense	make rebate
	pay compensation	pay donor	pay surcharge	pay fee	make debt	make purchase
	use material	use approach	use number	use one	make usage	make sort
make	use type	use method	use concept	use element	make placement	make size
use	use concept	use technique	use approach	use set	make kind	make utilization
	use form	use instrument	use method	use system	make quality	make redundancy
	use one	use system	use model	use type	make alternative	make handling

Table 6: Nearest neighbor verb-object phrases.

tion scores consistently improve when using the SVOPN data compared with using the SVO data, which shows using adjuncts is helpful in learning the meanings of verb phrases. Using the SVO data alone, verb phrase embeddings themselves are not directly learned but computed separately. By contrast, the SVOPN data provides the opportunity for learning verb phrase embeddings.

Effects of the training corpora. In previous work on learning and evaluating word embeddings, it is generally observed that increasing the training data results in better results. However, as opposed to our expectation, Table 4 and 5 show that using enWiki does not necessarily lead to better results. A possible explanation is that the nature of the training corpus matters the most. The usage of each word depends on the training corpora, and at least for these verb sense tasks, the size of BNC is sufficient and the nature of BNC fits these tasks.

4.1.3 Disambiguation Task

Our method outperforms both the baseline and the previous state of the art for GS'11, which demonstrates that our method better handles the disambiguation of transitive verbs. This result is somewhat expected since our method provides stronger interaction between predicates and their arguments than the baseline method.

Table 6 shows some examples[7] of verb-object phrases with their nearest neighbor ones in the embedding space according to the cosine similarity. For our method, we show the results of using the SVO and SVOPN data, and for PAS-CLBLM, we show the results of using the SVOPN data. In each setting, we used the enWiki data with $d = 50$.

Table 6 clearly shows the difference between our method and the baseline method. In our method, the meaning of "make" becomes close to those of "earn", "pay", and "use" when taking "money", "payment", and "use", respectively, as its object. By contrast, PAS-CLBLM simply emphasizes the head word "make". In previous work, it is also reported that the weighed addition composition functions put more weight on head words (Hashimoto et al., 2014; Muraoka et al., 2014; Socher et al., 2013). As opposed to these previous methods, our method has the ability of selecting the meaning of transitive verbs according to their objects.

Table 6 also shows that the phrase embeddings in our method are influenced by using the adjunct data (i.e., the SVOPN data). For example, in the example of "make money", the results for using the SVO data include "use money" as the nearest neighbors. When using the SVOPN data, the focus seems to shift to the true meaning of "make money".

4.1.4 Phrase Similarity Task

In the phrase similarity tasks, our method compares favorably to PAS-CLBLM for ML'10, but PAS-CLBLM outperforms our method for KS'13 and KS'14. These results are consistent with those in previous work. In Milajevs et al. (2014) and Polajnar et al. (2014), using the simplest composition function (the element-wise vector addition) achieves much better correlation scores than other tensor-based complex composition functions. These results indicate that our method is suitable for capturing the disambigua-

[7]The verb-object phrase "make use" is the part of the idiomatic expression "make use of".

Verb		Nearest neighbors
run	27th col.	operate, execute, insert, hold, grid, produce, add, assume, manage, render
	34th row	release, operate, create, override, govern, oversee, distribute, host, organize
	all	operate, start, manage, own, launch, continue, establish, open, maintain
encode	28th row	denature, transfect, phosphorylate, polymerize, subtend, acid
	39th row	format, store, decode, embed, concatenate, encrypt, memorize
	all	concatenate, permute, phosphorylate, quantize, composite, transfect, transduce

Table 7: Nearest neighbor verbs.

tion rather than capturing the topical similarity between phrases.

4.2 Qualitative Evaluation on Verb Matrices

Finally, we inspect the learned verb matrices using the SVO data of enWiki with $d = 50$. Compared with the word embeddings, the verb matrices have two-dimensional structure. According to Eq. (3), each row vector and each column vector in a verb matrix are updated to capture the information about what subject-object pairs are relevant (or irrelevant) to the verb.

Table 7 shows the nearest neighbor verbs using the cosine similarity between row (or column) vectors in the verb matrices. For reference, we also show the results using the vectorized representation of the verb matrices (denoted as "all" in the table). While the entire matrices capture the general similarity between verbs as with word embeddings, some specific rows (or columns) capture the multiple meanings of usages of the verbs.

5 Related Work

Based on the distributional hypothesis (Firth, 1957), various methods for word embeddings have been actively studied (Levy and Goldberg, 2014; Mikolov et al., 2013). Recent studies also investigate how to learn phrase and/or sentence embeddings using syntactic structures and word embeddings (Socher et al., 2011). Along the same line of research, there is a growing body of work on representing transitive verb phrases using word embeddings (Grefenstette and Sadrzadeh, 2011; Hashimoto et al., 2014; Kartsaklis et al., 2012; Tsubaki et al., 2013). Those studies can be split into two approaches: one is based on tensor calculus and the other is based on neural networks.

In contrast to the recent studies on word embeddings, the tensor-based methods represent words with tensors which are not limited to vectors. That is, higher order tensors such as matrices and three-mode tensors are also used. In the case of representing transitive verb phrases, for example, each transitive verb is represented as a matrix and each noun is represented as a vector in Grefenstette and Sadrzadeh (2011). Based on Coecke et al. (2010), Grefenstette and Sadrzadeh (2011) presented a method for calculating a verb matrix using word embeddings of its observed subjects and objects. The word embeddings were constructed by the method in Mitchell and Lapata (2008). Grefenstette and Sadrzadeh (2011) then introduced composition functions using the verb matrices and the noun embeddings. Their approach has been followed by some recent studies (Kartsaklis et al., 2012; Milajevs et al., 2014; Polajnar et al., 2014; Van de Cruys et al., 2013).

In the neural network-based methods each word is usually represented with a vector. Tsubaki et al. (2013) presented a neural network language model focusing on the binary relationship between verbs and their objects. Their co-compositionality method enables verb embeddings to be multiplicatively influenced by the objects, and vice versa. Subsequently, Hashimoto et al. (2014) introduced a method which jointly learns word and phrase embeddings by using a variety of predicate-argument structures. While their method achieves state-of-the-art results on phrase similarity tasks, the interaction between predicates and their arguments is weak.

6 Conclusion and Future Work

We have presented an implicit matrix factorization method for learning the embeddings of transitive verb phrases. The verb matrices learned by our method capture the multiple meanings of transitive verbs and we have shown that adjuncts play an important role in learning the meanings of transitive verb phrases. In our experiments, our method outperforms the previous state of the art on a transitive verb disambiguation task. In future work, we will investigate how the learned phrase embeddings improve real-world NLP applications.

Acknowledgments

We thank the anonymous reviewers for their helpful comments and suggestions.

References

Nathanael Chambers and Daniel Jurafsky. 2010. Improving the Use of Pseudo-Words for Evaluating Selectional Preferences. In *Proceedings of the 48th Annual Meeting of the Association for Computational Linguistics*, pages 445–453.

Bob Coecke, Mehrnoosh Sadrzadeh, and Stephen Clark. 2010. Mathematical Foundations for a Compositional Distributional Model of Meaning. *CoRR*, abs/1003.4394.

John Duchi, Elad Hazan, and Yoram Singer. 2011. Adaptive Subgradient Methods for Online Learning and Stochastic Optimization. *Journal of Machine Learning Research*, 12:2121–2159.

John Rupert Firth. 1957. A Synopsis of Linguistic Theory 1930-55. In *Studies in Linguistic Analysis*, pages 1–32.

Edward Grefenstette and Mehrnoosh Sadrzadeh. 2011. Experimental Support for a Categorical Compositional Distributional Model of Meaning. In *Proceedings of the 2011 Conference on Empirical Methods in Natural Language Processing*, pages 1394–1404.

Edward Grefenstette, Georgiana Dinu, Yao-Zhong Zhang, Mehrnoosh Sadrzadeh, and Marco Baroni. 2013. Multi-Step Regression Learning for Compositional Distributional Semantics. In *Proceedings of the 10th International Conference on Computational Semantics*, pages 131–142.

Kazuma Hashimoto, Pontus Stenetorp, Makoto Miwa, and Yoshimasa Tsuruoka. 2014. Jointly Learning Word Representations and Composition Functions Using Predicate-Argument Structures. In *Proceedings of the 2014 Conference on Empirical Methods in Natural Language Processing*, pages 1544–1555.

Karl Moritz Hermann and Phil Blunsom. 2013. The Role of Syntax in Vector Space Models of Compositional Semantics. In *Proceedings of the 51st Annual Meeting of the Association for Computational Linguistics (Volume 1: Long Papers)*, pages 894–904.

Dimitri Kartsaklis and Mehrnoosh Sadrzadeh. 2013. Prior Disambiguation of Word Tensors for Constructing Sentence Vectors. In *Proceedings of the 2013 Conference on Empirical Methods in Natural Language Processing*, pages 1590–1601.

Dimitri Kartsaklis and Mehrnoosh Sadrzadeh. 2014. A Study of Entanglement in a Categorical Framework of Natural Language. In *Proceedings of the 11th Workshop on Quantum Physics and Logic (QPL)*, Kyoto, Japan, June.

Dimitri Kartsaklis, Mehrnoosh Sadrzadeh, and Stephen Pulman. 2012. A Unified Sentence Space for Categorical Distributional-Compositional Semantics: Theory and Experiments. In *Proceedings of the 24th International Conference on Computational Linguistics*, pages 549–558.

Omer Levy and Yoav Goldberg. 2014. Neural Word Embedding as Implicit Matrix Factorization. In *Advances in Neural Information Processing Systems 27*, pages 2177–2185.

Tomas Mikolov, Ilya Sutskever, Kai Chen, Greg S Corrado, and Jeff Dean. 2013. Distributed Representations of Words and Phrases and their Compositionality. In *Advances in Neural Information Processing Systems 26*, pages 3111–3119.

Dmitrijs Milajevs, Dimitri Kartsaklis, Mehrnoosh Sadrzadeh, and Matthew Purver. 2014. Evaluating Neural Word Representations in Tensor-Based Compositional Settings. In *Proceedings of the 2014 Conference on Empirical Methods in Natural Language Processing*, pages 708–719.

Jeff Mitchell and Mirella Lapata. 2008. Vector-based Models of Semantic Composition. In *Proceedings of 46th Annual Meeting of the Association for Computational Linguistics: Human Language Technologies*, pages 236–244.

Jeff Mitchell and Mirella Lapata. 2010. Composition in Distributional Models of Semantics. *Cognitive Science*, 34(8):1388–1439.

Yusuke Miyao and Jun'ichi Tsujii. 2008. Feature forest models for probabilistic HPSG parsing. *Computational Linguistics*, 34(1):35–80, March.

Yusuke Miyao, Tomoko Ohta, Katsuya Masuda, Yoshimasa Tsuruoka, Kazuhiro Yoshida, Takashi Ninomiya, and Jun'ichi Tsujii. 2006. Semantic Retrieval for the Accurate Identification of Relational Concepts in Massive Textbases. In *Proceedings of the 21st International Conference on Computational Linguistics and 44th Annual Meeting of the Association for Computational Linguistics*, pages 1017–1024.

Masayasu Muraoka, Sonse Shimaoka, Kazeto Yamamoto, Yotaro Watanabe, Naoaki Okazaki, and Kentaro Inui. 2014. Finding The Best Model Among Representative Compositional Models. In *Proceedings of the 28th Pacific Asia Conference on Language, Information, and Computation*, pages 65–74.

Tamara Polajnar, Laura Rimell, and Stephen Clark. 2014. Using Sentence Plausibility to Learn the Semantics of Transitive Verbs. In *Proceedings of Workshop on Learning Semantics at the 2014 Conference on Neural Information Processing Systems.*

Richard Socher, Eric H. Huang, Jeffrey Pennin, Christopher D Manning, and Andrew Y. Ng. 2011. Dynamic Pooling and Unfolding Recursive Autoencoders for Paraphrase Detection. In *Advances in Neural Information Processing Systems 24*, pages 801–809.

Richard Socher, John Bauer, Christopher D. Manning, and Ng Andrew Y. 2013. Parsing with Compositional Vector Grammars. In *Proceedings of the*

51st Annual Meeting of the Association for Computational Linguistics (Volume 1: Long Papers), pages 455–465.

Rohini Srihari and Wel Li. 2000. A Question Answering System Supported by Information Extraction. In *Proceedings of the Sixth Conference on Applied Natural Language Processing*, pages 166–172.

Masashi Tsubaki, Kevin Duh, Masashi Shimbo, and Yuji Matsumoto. 2013. Modeling and Learning Semantic Co-Compositionality through Prototype Projections and Neural Networks. In *Proceedings of the 2013 Conference on Empirical Methods in Natural Language Processing*, pages 130–140.

Tim Van de Cruys, Thierry Poibeau, and Anna Korhonen. 2013. A Tensor-based Factorization Model of Semantic Compositionality. In *Proceedings of the 2013 Conference of the North American Chapter of the Association for Computational Linguistics: Human Language Technologies*, pages 1142–1151.

Tim Van de Cruys. 2014. A Neural Network Approach to Selectional Preference Acquisition. In *Proceedings of the 2014 Conference on Empirical Methods in Natural Language Processing*, pages 26–35.

Recursive Neural Networks Can Learn Logical Semantics

Samuel R. Bowman[*†] **Christopher Potts**[*] **Christopher D. Manning**[*†‡]
sbowman@stanford.edu cgpotts@stanford.edu manning@stanford.edu

{[*]Dept. of Linguistics, [†]NLP Group, [‡]Dept. of Computer Science}
Stanford University
Stanford, CA 94305, USA

Abstract

Tree-structured recursive neural networks (TreeRNNs) for sentence meaning have been successful for many applications, but it remains an open question whether the fixed-length representations that they learn can support tasks as demanding as logical deduction. We pursue this question by evaluating whether two such models—plain TreeRNNs and tree-structured neural tensor networks (TreeRNTNs)—can correctly learn to identify logical relationships such as entailment and contradiction using these representations. In our first set of experiments, we generate artificial data from a logical grammar and use it to evaluate the models' ability to learn to handle basic relational reasoning, recursive structures, and quantification. We then evaluate the models on the more natural SICK challenge data. Both models perform competitively on the SICK data and generalize well in all three experiments on simulated data, suggesting that they can learn suitable representations for logical inference in natural language.

1 Introduction

Tree-structured recursive neural network models (TreeRNNs; Goller and Kuchler 1996; Socher et al. 2011b) for sentence meaning have been successful in an array of sophisticated language tasks, including sentiment analysis (Socher et al., 2011b; Irsoy and Cardie, 2014), image description (Socher et al., 2014), and paraphrase detection (Socher et al., 2011a). These results are encouraging for the ability of these models to learn to produce and use strong semantic representations for sentences. However, it remains an open question whether any such fully learned model can achieve the kind of high-fidelity distributed representations proposed in recent algebraic work on vector space modeling (Coecke et al., 2011; Grefenstette, 2013; Hermann et al., 2013; Rocktäschel et al., 2014), and whether any such model can match the performance of grammars based in logical forms in their ability to model core semantic phenomena like quantification, entailment, and contradiction (Warren and Pereira, 1982; Zelle and Mooney, 1996; Zettlemoyer and Collins, 2005; Liang et al., 2013).

Recent work on the algebraic approach of Coecke et al. (2011) has yielded rich frameworks for computing the meanings of fragments of natural language compositionally from vector or tensor representations, but has not yet yielded effective methods for learning these representations from data in typical machine learning settings. Past experimental work on reasoning with distributed representations have been largely confined to short phrases (Mitchell and Lapata, 2010; Grefenstette et al., 2011; Baroni et al., 2012). However, for robust natural language understanding, it is essential to model these phenomena in their full generality on complex linguistic structures.

This paper describes four machine learning experiments that directly evaluate the abilities of these models to learn representations that support specific semantic behaviors. These tasks follow the format of *natural language inference* (also known as *recognizing textual entailment*; Dagan et al. 2006), in which the goal is to determine the core inferential relationship between two sentences. We introduce a novel NN architecture for natural language inference which independently computes vector representations for each of two sentences using standard TreeRNN or TreeRNTN (Socher et al., 2013) models, and produces a judgment for the pair using only those representations. This allows us to gauge the abilities of these two models to represent all of the necessary semantic

Proceedings of the 3rd Workshop on Continuous Vector Space Models and their Compositionality (CVSC), pages 12–21,
Beijing, China, July 26-31, 2015. ©2015 Association for Computational Linguistics

information in the sentence vectors.

Much of the theoretical work on natural language inference (and some successful implemented models; MacCartney and Manning 2009; Watanabe et al. 2012) involves *natural logics*, which are formal systems that define rules of inference between natural language words, phrases, and sentences without the need of intermediate representations in an artificial logical language. In our first three experiments, we test our models' ability to learn the foundations of natural language inference by training them to reproduce the behavior of the natural logic of MacCartney and Manning (2009) on artificial data. This logic defines seven mutually-exclusive relations of synonymy, entailment, contradiction, and mutual consistency, as summarized in Table 1, and it provides rules of semantic combination for projecting these relations from the lexicon up to complex phrases. The formal properties of this system are now well-understood (Icard and Moss, 2013a; Icard and Moss, 2013b). The first experiment using this logic covers reasoning with the bare logical relations (§3), the second extends this to reasoning with statements constructed compositionally from recursive functions (§4), and the third covers the additional complexity that results from quantification (§5). Though the performance of the plain TreeRNN model is somewhat poor in our first experiment, we find that the stronger TreeRNTN model generalizes well in every case, suggesting that it has learned to simulate our target logical concepts.

The experiments with simulated data provide a convincing demonstration of the ability of neural networks to learn to build and use semantic representations for complex natural language sentences from reasonably-sized training sets. However, we are also interested in the more practical question of whether they can learn these representations from naturalistic text. To address this question, we apply our models to the SICK entailment challenge data in §6. The small size of this corpus puts data-hungry NN models like ours at a disadvantage, but we are nonetheless able to achieve competitive performance on it, surpassing several submitted models with significant hand-engineered task-specific features and our own NN baseline. This suggests that the representational abilities that we observe in the previous sections are not limited to carefully circumscribed tasks. We conclude that TreeRNTN models are adequate for typical cases of natural language inference, and that there is not yet any clear level of inferential complexity for which other approaches work and NN models fail.

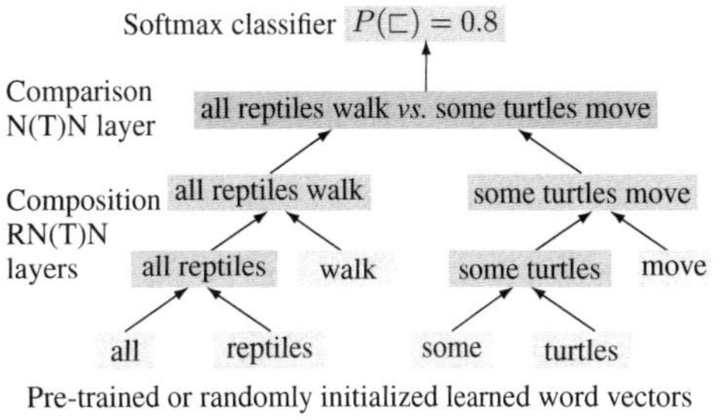

Figure 1: In our model, two separate tree-structured networks build up vector representations for each of two sentences using either NN or NTN layer functions. A comparison layer then uses the resulting vectors to produce features for a classifier.

2 Tree-structured neural networks

We limit the scope of our experiments in this paper to neural network models that adhere to the linguistic *principle of compositionality*, which says that the meanings for complex expressions are derived from the meanings of their parts via specific composition functions (Partee, 1984; Janssen, 1997). In our distributed setting, word meanings are embedding vectors of dimension N. A learned composition function maps pairs of them to single phrase vectors of dimension N, which can then be merged again to represent more complex phrases, forming a tree structure. Once the entire sentence-level representation has been derived at the top of the tree, it serves as a fixed-dimensional input for some subsequent layer function.

To apply these recursive models to our task, we propose the tree pair model architecture depicted in Fig. 1. In it, the two phrases being compared are processed separately using a pair of tree-structured networks that share a single set of parameters. The resulting vectors are fed into a separate comparison layer that is meant to generate a feature vector capturing the relation between the two phrases. The output of this layer is then given to a softmax classifier, which produces a distribution over the seven relations represented in Table 1.

For the sentence embedding portions of the network, we evaluate both TreeRNN models with the

Name	Symbol	Set-theoretic definition	Example
(strict) entailment	$x \sqsubset y$	$x \subset y$	*turtle, reptile*
(strict) reverse entailment	$x \sqsupset y$	$x \supset y$	*reptile, turtle*
equivalence	$x \equiv y$	$x = y$	*couch, sofa*
alternation	$x \mid y$	$x \cap y = \emptyset \wedge x \cup y \neq \mathcal{D}$	*turtle, warthog*
negation	$x \wedge y$	$x \cap y = \emptyset \wedge x \cup y = \mathcal{D}$	*able, unable*
cover	$x \smile y$	$x \cap y \neq \emptyset \wedge x \cup y = \mathcal{D}$	*animal, non-turtle*
independence	$x \# y$	(else)	*turtle, pet*

Table 1: The seven relations of MacCartney and Manning (2009)'s logic are defined abstractly on pairs of sets drawing from the universe $\mathcal{D}$, but can be straightforwardly applied to any pair of natural language words, phrases, or sentences. The relations are defined so as to be mutually exclusive.

standard NN layer function (1) and those with the more powerful neural tensor network layer function (2) proposed in Chen et al. (2013). The nonlinearity $f(x) = \tanh(x)$ is applied elementwise to the output of either layer function.

$$(1)\quad \vec{y}_{TreeRNN} = f(\mathbf{M}\begin{bmatrix}\vec{x}^{(l)}\\ \vec{x}^{(r)}\end{bmatrix} + \vec{b})$$

$$(2)\quad \vec{y}_{TreeRNTN} = \vec{y}_{TreeRNN} + f(\vec{x}^{(l)T}\mathbf{T}^{[1\ldots n]}\vec{x}^{(r)})$$

Here, $\vec{x}^{(l)}$ and $\vec{x}^{(r)}$ are the column vector representations for the left and right children of the node, and $\vec{y}$ is the node's output. The TreeRNN concatenates them, multiplies them by an $N \times 2N$ matrix of learned weights, and adds a bias $\vec{b}$. The TreeRNTN adds a learned full rank third-order tensor $\mathbf{T}$, of dimension $N \times N \times N$, modeling multiplicative interactions between the child vectors. The comparison layer uses the same layer function as the composition layers (either an NN layer or an NTN layer) with independently learned parameters and a separate nonlinearity function. Rather than use a tanh nonlinearity here, we found better results with the leaky rectified linear function (Maas et al., 2013): $f(x) = \max(x, 0) + 0.01\min(x, 0)$.

Other strong tree-structured models have been proposed in past work (Socher et al., 2014; Irsoy and Cardie, 2014; Tai et al., 2015), but we believe that these two provide a valuable case study, and that positive results on here are likely to generalize well to stronger models.

To run the model forward, we assemble the two tree-structured networks so as to match the structures provided for each phrase, which are either included in the source data or given by a parser. The word vectors are then looked up from the vocabulary embedding matrix V (one of the learned model parameters), and the composition and comparison functions are used to pass information up the tree and into the classifier. For an objective function, we use the negative log likelihood of the correct label with tuned L2 regularization.

We initialize parameters uniformly, using the range $(-0.05, 0.05)$ for layer parameters and $(-0.01, 0.01)$ for embeddings, and train the model using stochastic gradient descent (SGD) with learning rates computed using AdaDelta (Zeiler, 2012). The classifier feature vector is fixed at 75 dimensions and the dimensions of the recursive layers are tuned manually. Training times on CPUs vary from hours to days across experiments. On the experiments which use artificial data, we report mean results over five fold cross-validation, where variance across runs is typically no more than two percentage points. In addition, because the classes are not necessarily balanced, we report both accuracy and macroaveraged F1.[1] Source code and generated data can be downloaded from `http://stanford.edu/~sbowman/`.

3 Reasoning about semantic relations

The simplest kinds of deduction in natural logic involve atomic statements using the relations in Table 1. For instance, from the relation $p_1 \sqsupset p_2$ between two propositions, one can infer the relation $p_2 \sqsubset p_1$ by applying the definitions of the relations directly. If one is also given the relation $p_2 \sqsupset p_3$ one can conclude that $p_1 \sqsupset p_3$, by basic set-theoretic reasoning (transitivity of $\sqsupset$). The full set of sound such inferences on pairs of premise relations is depicted in Table 2. Though these basic inferences do not involve compositional sentence representations, any successful reasoning using compositional representations will rely on the ability to perform sound inferences of this kind

[1] We compute macroaveraged F1 as the harmonic mean of average precision and average recall, both computed for all classes for which there is test data, setting precision to 0 where it is not defined.

	$\equiv$	$\sqsubset$	$\sqsupset$	$\wedge$	$\mid$	$\smile$	$\#$
$\equiv$	$\equiv$	$\sqsubset$	$\sqsupset$	$\wedge$	$\mid$	$\smile$	$\#$
$\sqsubset$	$\sqsubset$	$\sqsubset$	·	$\mid$	$\mid$	·	·
$\sqsupset$	$\sqsupset$	·	$\sqsupset$	$\smile$	·	$\smile$	·
$\wedge$	$\wedge$	$\smile$	$\mid$	$\equiv$	$\sqsupset$	$\sqsubset$	$\#$
$\mid$	$\mid$	·	$\mid$	$\sqsubset$	·	$\sqsubset$	·
$\smile$	$\smile$	$\smile$	·	$\sqsupset$	$\sqsupset$	·	·
$\#$	$\#$	·	·	$\#$	·	·	·

Table 2: In §3, we assess our models' ability to learn to do inference over pairs of relations using the rules represented here, which are derived from the definitions of the relations in Table 1. As an example, given that $p_1 \sqsubset p_2$ and $p_2 \wedge p_3$, the entry in the $\sqsubset$ row and the $\wedge$ column lets us conclude that $p_1 \mid p_3$. Cells containing a dot correspond to situations for which no valid inference can be drawn.

	Train	Test
# only	53.8 (10.5)	53.8 (10.5)
15d NN	99.8 (99.0)	94.0 (87.0)
15d NTN	**100 (100)**	**99.6 (95.5)**

Table 3: Performance on the semantic relation experiments. These results and all other results on artificial data are reported as mean accuracy scores over five runs followed by mean macroaveraged F1 scores in parentheses. The "# only" entries reflect the frequency of the most frequent class.

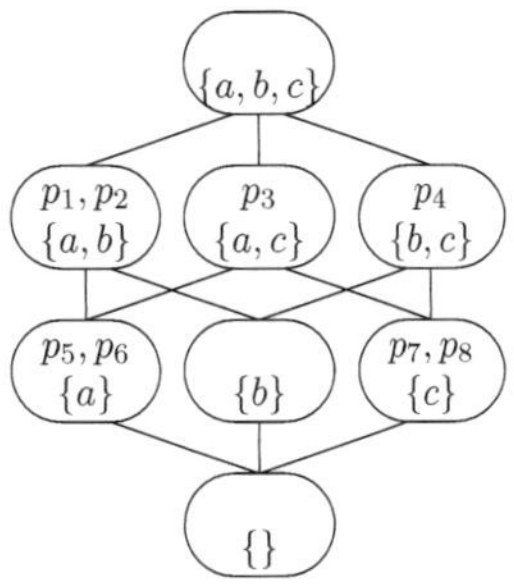

(a) Example boolean structure, shown with edges idicating inclusion. The terms p_1–p_8 name the sets. Not all sets have names, and some sets have multiple names, so that learning $\equiv$ is non-trivial.

Train	Test
$p_1 \equiv p_2$	$p_2 \wedge p_7$
$p_1 \sqsupset p_5$	$p_2 \sqsupset p_5$
$p_4 \sqsupset p_8$	~~$p_5 \equiv p_6$~~
$p_5 \mid p_7$	~~$p_7 \sqsubset p_4$~~
$p_7 \wedge p_1$	$p_8 \sqsubset p_4$

(b) A few examples of atomic statements about the model depicted above. Test statements that are not provable from the training data shown are crossed out.

Figure 2: Small example structure and data for learning relation composition.

in order to be able to use unseen relational facts within larger derivations. Our first experiment studies how well each model can learn to perform them them in isolation.

Experiments We begin by creating a world model on which we will base the statements in the train and test sets. This takes the form of a small Boolean structure in which terms denote sets of entities from a small domain. Fig. 2a depicts a structure of this form with three entities (a, b, and c) and eight proposition terms (p_1–p_8). We then generate a relational statement for each pair of terms in the model, as shown in Fig. 2b. We divide these statements evenly into train and test sets, and delete the test set examples which cannot be proven from the train examples, for which there is not enough information for even an ideal system to choose a correct label. In each experimental run, we create a model with 80 terms over a domain of 7 elements, yielding a training set of 3200 examples and a test set of 2960 examples.

We trained models with both the NN and NTN comparison functions on these data sets.[2] In both cases, the models are implemented as described in §2, but since the items being compared are single terms rather than full tree structures, the composition layer is not used, and the two models are not recursive. We simply present the models with the (randomly initialized) embedding vectors for each of two terms, ensuring that the model has no information about the terms being compared except for the relations between them that appear in training.

Results The results (Table 3) show that NTN is able to accurately encode the relations between the terms in the geometric relations between their vectors, and is able to then use that information to recover relations that are not overtly included in the training data. The NN also generalizes fairly well, but makes enough errors that it remains an open question whether it is capable of learning representations with these properties. It is not possible for us to rule out the possibility that different optimization techniques or finer-grained hyperparameter tuning could lead an NN model to succeed.

As an example from our test data, both mod-

[2]Since this task relies crucially on the learning of a pair of vectors, no simpler version of our model is a viable baseline.

els correctly labeled $p_1 \sqsubset p_3$, potentially learning from the training examples $\{p_1 \sqsubset p_{51},\ p_3 \sqsupset p_{51}\}$ or $\{p_1 \sqsubset p_{65},\ p_3 \sqsupset p_{65}\}$. On another example involving comparably frequent relations, the NTN correctly labeled $p_6 \sqsupset p_{24}$, likely on the basis of the training examples $\{p_6 \smile p_{28},\ p_{28} \wedge p_{24}\}$, while the NN incorrectly assigned it $\#$.

4 Recursive structure

A successful natural language inference system must reason about relations not just over familiar atomic symbols, but also over novel structures built up recursively from these symbols. This section shows that our models can learn a compositional semantics over such structures. In our evaluations, we exploit the fact that our logical language is infinite by testing on strings that are longer and more complex than any seen in training.

Experiments As in §3, we generate artificial data from a formal system, but we now replace the unanalyzed symbols from that experiment with complex formulae. These formulae represent a complete classical propositional logic: each atomic symbol is a variable over the domain $\{\texttt{T}, \texttt{F}\}$, and the only operators are truth-functional ones. Table 4a defines this logic, and Table 4b gives some short examples of relational statements from our data. To compute these relations between statements, we exhaustively enumerate the sets of assignments of truth values to propositional variables that would satisfy each of the statements, and then we convert the set-theoretic relation between those assignments into one of the seven relations in Table 1. As a result, each relational statement represents a valid theorem of the propositional logic, and to succeed, the models must learn to reproduce the behavior of a theorem prover.[3]

In our experiments, we randomly generate unique pairs of formulae containing up to 12 instances of logical operators each and compute the relation that holds for each pair. We discard pairs in which either statement is either a tautology or a contradiction, for which the seven relations in Table 1 are undefined. The resulting set of formula pairs is then partitioned into 12 bins according the number of operators in the larger of the two formulae. We then sample 20% of each bin for a held-out test set. If we do not implement any constraint that the two statements being compared are similar in any way, then the generated data are dominated by statements in which the two formulae refer to largely separate subsets of the six variables, which means that the $\#$ relation is almost always correct. In an effort to balance the distribution of relation labels without departing from the basic task of modeling propositional logic, we disallow individual pairs of statements from referring to more than four of the six propositional variables.

In order to test the model's generalization to unseen structures, we discard training examples with more than 4 logical operators, yielding 60k short training examples, and 21k test examples across all 12 bins. In addition to the two tree models, we also train a summing NN baseline which is largely identical to the TreeRNN, except that instead of using a learned composition function, it simply sums the term vectors in each expression to compose them before passing them to the comparison layer. Unlike the two tree models, this baseline does not use word order, and is as such guaranteed to ignore some information that it would need in order to succeed perfectly.

Results Fig. 3 shows the relationship between test accuracy and statement size. While the summing baseline model performed poorly across the

Formula	Interpretation
$p_1, p_2, p_3, p_4, p_5, p_6$	$[\![x]\!] \in \{\texttt{T}, \texttt{F}\}$
$\textit{not}\ \varphi$	$\texttt{T}$ iff $[\![\varphi]\!] = \texttt{F}$
$(\varphi\ \textit{and}\ \psi)$	$\texttt{T}$ iff $\texttt{F} \notin \{[\![\varphi]\!], [\![\psi]\!]\}$
$(\varphi\ \textit{or}\ \psi)$	$\texttt{T}$ iff $\texttt{T} \in \{[\![\varphi]\!], [\![\psi]\!]\}$

(a) Well-formed formulae. φ and ψ range over all well-formed formulae, and $[\![\cdot]\!]$ is the interpretation function mapping formulae into $\{\texttt{T}, \texttt{F}\}$.

$\textit{not}\ p_3$	$\wedge$	p_3
$\textit{not not}\ p_6$	$\equiv$	p_6
p_3	$\sqsubset$	$(p_3\ \textit{or}\ p_2)$
$(p_1\ \textit{or}\ (p_2\ \textit{or}\ p_4))$	$\sqsupset$	$(p_2\ \textit{and not}\ p_4)$
$\textit{not}\ (\textit{not}\ p_1\ \textit{and not}\ p_2)$	$\equiv$	$(p_1\ \textit{or}\ p_2)$

(b) Short examples of the type of statements used for training and testing. These are relations between well-formed formulae, computed in terms of sets of satisfying interpretation functions $[\![\cdot]\!]$.

Table 4: Natural logic relations over sentences of propositional logic.

[3] Socher et al. (2012) show that a matrix-vector TreeRNN model somewhat similar to our TreeRNTN can learn boolean logic, a logic where the atomic symbols are simply the values T and F. While learning the operators of that logic is not trivial, the outputs of each operator can be represented accurately by a single bit. In the much more demanding task presented here, the atomic symbols are variables over these values, and the sentence vectors must thus be able to distinguish up to 2^{2^6} distinct conditions on valuations.

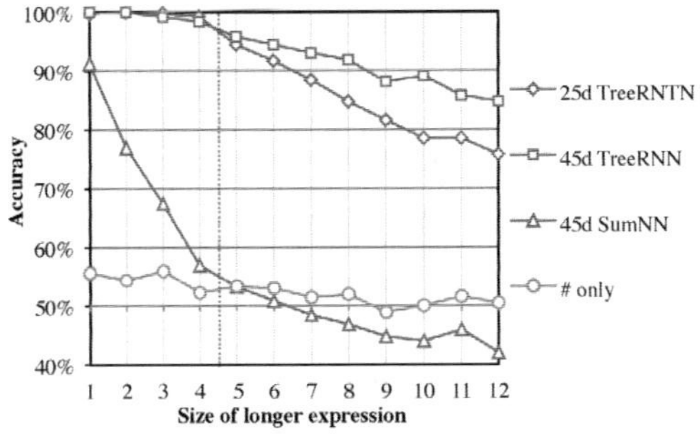

Figure 3: Results on recursive structure. The vertical dotted line marks the size of the longest training examples.

board, we found that both recursive models were able to perform well on unseen small test examples, with TreeRNN accuracy above 98% and TreeRNTN accuracy above 99% on formulae below length five, indicating that they learned correct approximations of the underlying logic. Training accuracy was 66.6% for the SumNN, 99.4% for the TreeRNN, and 99.8% for the TreeRNTN.

After the size four training cutoff, performance gradually decays with expression size for both tree models, suggesting that the learned approximations were accurate but lossy. Despite the TreeRNTN's stronger performance on short sentences, its performance decayed more quickly than the TreeRNN's. This suggests to us that it learned to interpret many specific fixed-size tree structures directly, allowing it to get away without learning as robust generalizations about how to compose terms in the general case. Two factors may have contributed to the learning of these narrower generalizations: even with the lower dimension, the TreeRNTN composition function has about eight times as many parameters as the TreeRNN, and the TreeRNTN worked best with weaker L2 regularization than the TreeRNN ($\lambda = 0.0003$ vs. 0.001). However, even in the most complex set of test examples, the TreeRNTN classifies true examples of every class but $\equiv$ (which is rare in long examples, and occurs only once here) correctly the majority of the time, and the performance of both models on those examples indicates that both have learned reasonable approximations of the underlying theorem proving task over recursive structure.

5 Reasoning with quantifiers and negation

We have seen that recursive models can learn an approximation of propositional logic. However, natural languages can express functional meanings of considerably greater complexity than this. As a key test of whether our models can capture this complexity, we now study the degree to which they are able to develop suitable representations for the semantics of natural language quantifiers like *most* and *all* as they interact with negation and lexical entailments. Quantification and negation are far from the only place in natural language where complex functional meanings are found, but they are natural focus, since they have formed a standard case study in prior formal work on natural language inference (Icard and Moss, 2013b).

Experiments Our data consist of pairs of sentences generated from a grammar for a simple English-like artificial language. Each sentence contains a quantifier, a noun which may be negated, and an intransitive verb which may be negated. We use the quantifiers *some*, *most*, *all*, *two*, and *three*, and their negations *no*, *not-all*, *not-most*, *less-than-two*, and *less-than-three*, and also include five nouns, four intransitive verbs, and the negation symbol *not*. In order to be able to define relations between sentences with differing lexical items, we define the lexical relations for each noun–noun pair, each verb–verb pair, and each quantifier–quantifier pair. The grammar then generates pairs of sentences and calculates the relations between them. For instance, our models might then see pairs like (3) and (4) in training and be required to then label (5).

(3) (most turtle) swim | (no turtle) move

(4) (all lizard) reptile $\sqsubset$ (some lizard) animal

(5) (most turtle) reptile | (all turtle) (not animal)

In each run, we randomly partition the set of valid *single sentences* into train and test, and then label all of the pairs from within each set to generate a training set of 27k pairs and a test set of 7k pairs. Because the model doesn't see the test sentences at training time, it cannot directly use the kind of reasoning described in §3 at the sentence level (by treating sentences as unanalyzed symbols), and must instead jointly learn the word-level relations and a complete reasoning system over them for our logic.

	Train	Test
# only	35.4 (7.5)	35.4 (7.5)
25d SumNN	96.9 (97.7)	93.9 (95.0)
25d TreeRNN	99.6 (99.6)	99.2 (99.3)
25d TreeRNTN	**100** (**100**)	**99.7** (**99.5**)

Table 5: Performance on the quantifier experiments, given as % correct and macroaveraged F1.

We use the same summing baseline as in §4. The highly consistent sentence structure in this experiment means that this model is not as disadvantaged by the lack of word order information as it is in the previous experiment, but the variable placement of *not* nonetheless introduces potential uncertainty in the 58.8% of examples that contain a sentence with a single token of it.

Results The results (Table 5) show that both tree models are able to learn to generalize the underlying logic almost perfectly. The baseline summing model can largely memorize the training data, but does not generalize as well. We do not find any consistent pattern in the handful of errors made by either tree model, and no errors were consistent across model restarts, suggesting that there is no fundamental obstacle to learning a perfect model for this problem.

6 The SICK textual entailment challenge

The specific model architecture that we use is novel, and though the underlying tree structure approach has been validated elsewhere, our experiments so far do not guarantee that it viable model for handling inference over real natural language data. To investigate our models' ability to handle the noisy labels and the diverse range of linguistic structures seen in typical natural language data, we use the SICK textual entailment challenge corpus (Marelli et al., 2014b). The corpus consists of about 10k natural language sentence pairs, labeled with *entailment*, *contradiction*, or *neutral*. At only a few thousand distinct sentences (many of them variants on an even smaller set of template sentences), the corpus is not large enough to train a high quality learned model of general natural language, but it is the largest human-labeled entailment corpus that we are aware of, and our results nonetheless show that tree-structured NN models can learn to approximate natural logic-style inference in the real world.

Adapting to this task requires us to make a few additions to the techniques discussed in §2. In order to better handle rare words, we initialized our word embeddings using 200 dimensional vectors trained with GloVe (Pennington et al., 2014) on data from Wikipedia. Since 200 dimensional vectors are too large to be practical in an TreeRNTN on a small dataset, a new embedding transformation layer is needed. Before any embedding is used as an input to a recursive layer, it is passed through an additional tanh neural network layer with the same output dimension as the recursive layer. This new layer allows the model to choose which aspects of the 200 dimensional representations from the unsupervised source it most values, rather than relying on GloVe—which is has no knowledge of the task—to do so, as would be the case were GloVe asked to directly produce vectors of the lower dimensionality. An identical layer is added to the SumNN between the word vectors and the comparison layer.

We also supplemented the SICK training data[4] (4500 examples) with 600k examples of approximate entailment data from the Denotation Graph project (DG, Hodosh et al. 2014, also used by the winning SICK submission), a corpus of noisy automatically labeled entailment examples over image captions, the same genre of text from which SICK was drawn. We trained a single model on data from both sources, but used a separate set of softmax parameters for classifying into the labels from each source, and forced the model to sample SICK examples and DG examples about equally often during training.

We parsed the data from both sources with the Stanford PCFG Parser v. 3.3.1 (Klein and Manning, 2003). We also found that we were able to train a working model much more quickly with an additional technique: we collapse subtrees that were identical across both sentences in a pair by replacing them with a single head word. The training and test data on which we report performance are collapsed in this way, and both collapsed and uncollapsed copies of the training data are used in training. Finally, in order to improve regularization on the noisier data, we used dropout (Srivastava et al., 2014) at the input to the comparison layer (10%) and at the output from the embedding

[4]We tuned the model using performance on a held out development set, but report performance here for a version of the model trained on both the training and development data and tested on the 4,928 example SICK test set. We also report training accuracy on a small sample from each data source.

The patient is being helped by the doctor	*entailment*	The doctor is helping the patient (PASSIVE)
A little girl is playing the violin on a beach	*contradiction*	There is no girl playing the violin on a beach (NEG)
The yellow dog is drinking water from a bottle	*contradiction*	The yellow dog is drinking water from a pot (SUBST)
A woman is breaking two eggs in a bowl	*neutral*	A man is mixing a few ingredients in a bowl (MULTIED)
Dough is being spread by a man	*neutral*	A woman is slicing meat with a knife (DIFF)

Table 6: Examples of each category used in error analysis from the SICK test data.

	neutral only	30d SumNN	30d TrRNN	50d TrRNTN
DG Train	50.0	68.0	67.0	**74.0**
SICK Train	56.7	96.6	95.4	**97.8**
SICK Test	56.7	73.4	74.9	**76.9**
PASSIVE (4%)	0	76	68	**88**
NEG (7%)	0	96	**100**	**100**
SUBST (24%)	28	**72**	64	**72**
MULTIED (39%)	**68**	61	66	64
DIFF (26%)	**96**	68	79	**96**
SHORT (47%)	50.0	73.9	73.5	**77.3**

Table 7: Classification accuracy, including a category breakdown for SICK test data. Categories are shown with their frequencies.

transform layer (25%).

Results Despite the small amount of high quality training data available and the lack of resources for learning lexical relationships, the results (Table 7) show that our tree-structured models perform competitively on textual entailment, beating a strong baseline. Neither model reached the performance of the winning system (84.6%), but the TreeRNTN did exceed that of eight out of 18 submitted systems, including several which used sophisticated hand-engineered features and lexical resources specific to the version of the entailment task at hand.

To better understand our results, we manually annotated a fraction of the SICK test set, using mutually exclusive categories for passive/active alternation pairs (PASSIVE), pairs differing only by the presence of negation (NEG), pairs differing by a single word or phrase substitution (SUBST), pairs differing by multiple edits (MULTIED), and pairs with little or no content word overlap (DIFF). Examples of each are in Table 6. We annotated 100 random examples to judge the frequency of each category, and continued selectively annotating until each category contained at least 25. We also use the category SHORT for pairs in which neither sentence contains more than ten words.

The results (Table 7) show that the TreeRNTN performs especially strongly in the two categories which pick out specific syntactic configurations, PASSIVE and NEG, suggesting that that model has learned to encode the relevant structures well. It also performs fairly on SUBST, which most closely parallels the lexical entailment inferences addressed in §5. In addition, none of the models perform dramatically better on the SHORT pairs than on the rest of the data, suggesting that the performance decay observed in §4 may not impact models trained on typical natural language text.

It is known that a model can perform well on SICK (like other natural language inference corpora) without taking advantage of compositional syntactic or semantic structure (Marelli et al., 2014a), and our summing baseline model is powerful enough to do this. Our tree models nonetheless perform substantially better, and we remain confident that given sufficient data, it should be possible for the tree models, and not the summing model, to learn a truly high-quality solution.

7 Discussion and conclusion

This paper first evaluates two recursive models on three natural language inference tasks over clean artificial data, covering the core relational algebra of natural logic with entailment and exclusion, recursive structure, and quantification. We then show that the same models can learn to perform an entailment task on natural language. The results suggest that TreeRNTNs, and potentially also TreeRNNs, can learn to faithfully reproduce logical inference behaviors from reasonably-sized training sets. These positive results are promising for the future of learned representation models in the applied modeling of compositional semantics.

Some questions about the abilities of these models remain open. Even the TreeRNTN falls short of perfection in the recursion experiment, with performance falling off steadily as the size of the expressions grows. It remains to be seen whether these deficiencies are limiting in practice, and whether they can be overcome with stronger models or learning techniques. In addition, interesting analytical questions remain about *how* these models encode the underlying logics. Neither the underlying logical theories, nor any straightforward parameter inspection technique provides much insight on this point, but we hope that further experiments may reveal structure in the learned parameters or the representations they produce.

Our SICK experiments similarly only begin to reveal the potential of these models to learn to perform complex semantic inferences from corpora, and there is ample room to develop our understanding using new and larger sources of natural language data. Nonetheless, the rapid progress the field has made with these models in recent years provides ample reason to be optimistic that learned representation models can be trained to meet all the challenges of natural language semantics.

Acknowledgments

We thank Jeffrey Pennington and Richard Socher, as well as Neha Nayak for developing the SICK collapsing technique.

We also gratefully acknowledge support from a Google Faculty Research Award, a gift from Bloomberg L.P., the Defense Advanced Research Projects Agency (DARPA) Deep Exploration and Filtering of Text (DEFT) Program under Air Force Research Laboratory (AFRL) contract no. FA8750-13-2-0040, the National Science Foundation under grant no. IIS 1159679, and the Department of the Navy, Office of Naval Research, under grant no. N00014-10-1-0109. Any opinions, findings, and conclusions or recommendations expressed in this material are those of the authors and do not necessarily reflect the views of Google, Bloomberg L.P., DARPA, AFRL NSF, ONR, or the US government.

References

M. Baroni, R. Bernardi, N.Q. Do, and C.C. Shan. 2012. Entailment above the word level in distributional semantics. In *Proc. EACL*.

D. Chen, R. Socher, C.D. Manning, and A.Y. Ng. 2013. Learning new facts from knowledge bases with neural tensor networks and semantic word vectors. In *Proc. ICLR*.

B. Coecke, M. Sadrzadeh, and S. Clark. 2011. Mathematical foundations for a compositional distributed model of meaning. *Linguistic Analysis*, 36(1–4).

I. Dagan, O. Glickman, and B. Magnini. 2006. The PASCAL Recognising Textual Entailment Challenge. In *Machine Learning Challenges. Evaluating Predictive Uncertainty, Visual Object Classification, and Recognising Tectual Entailment*. Springer.

C. Goller and A. Kuchler. 1996. Learning task-dependent distributed representations by backpropagation through structure. In *Proc. IEEE International Conference on Neural Networks*.

E. Grefenstette, M. Sadrzadeh, S. Clark, B. Coecke, and S. Pulman. 2011. Concrete sentence spaces for compositional distributional models of meaning. In *Proc. IWCS*.

E. Grefenstette. 2013. Towards a formal distributional semantics: Simulating logical calculi with tensors. In *Proc. *SEM*.

K.M. Hermann, E. Grefenstette, and P. Blunsom. 2013. "Not not bad" is not "bad": A distributional account of negation. In *Proc. of the 2013 Workshop on Continuous Vector Space Models and their Compositionality*.

M. Hodosh, P. Young, A. Lai, and J. Hockenmaier. 2014. From image descriptions to visual denotations: New similarity metrics for semantic inference over event descriptions. *TACL*.

T.F. Icard and L.S. Moss. 2013a. A complete calculus of monotone and antitone higher-order functions. In N. Galatos, A. Kurz, and C. Tsinakis, editors, *Proc. Topology, Algebra, and Categories in Logic*.

T.F. Icard and L.S. Moss. 2013b. Recent progress on monotonicity. *LILT*, 9(7).

O. Irsoy and C. Cardie. 2014. Deep recursive neural networks for compositionality in language. In *Proc. NIPS*.

T.M.V. Janssen. 1997. Compositionality. In J. van Benthem and A. ter Meulen, editors, *Handbook of Logic and Language*. MIT Press and North-Holland.

D. Klein and C.D. Manning. 2003. Accurate unlexicalized parsing. In *Proc. ACL*.

P. Liang, M.I. Jordan, and D. Klein. 2013. Learning dependency-based compositional semantics. *Computational Linguistics*, 39(2).

A.L. Maas, A.Y. Hannun, and A.Y. Ng. 2013. Rectifier nonlinearities improve neural network acoustic models. In *Proc. ICML*.

B. MacCartney and C.D. Manning. 2009. An extended model of natural logic. In *Proc. IWCS*.

M. Marelli, L. Bentivogli, M. Baroni, R. Bernardi, S. Menini, and R. Zamparelli. 2014a. SemEval-2014 task 1: Evaluation of compositional distributional semantic models on full sentences through semantic relatedness and textual entailment. *SemEval-2014*.

M. Marelli, S. Menini, M. Baroni, L. Bentivogli, R. Bernardi, and R. Zamparelli. 2014b. A SICK cure for the evaluation of compositional distributional semantic models. In *Proc. LREC*.

J. Mitchell and M. Lapata. 2010. Composition in distributional models of semantics. *Cognitive Science*, 34(8).

B.H. Partee. 1984. Compositionality. In Fred Landman and Frank Veltman, editors, *Varieties of Formal Semantics*. Foris.

J. Pennington, R. Socher, and C.D. Manning. 2014. GloVe: Global vectors for word representation. In *Proc. EMNLP*.

T. Rocktäschel, M. Bosnjak, S. Singh, and S. Riedel. 2014. Low-dimensional embeddings of logic. In *Proc. the ACL 2014 Workshop on Semantic Parsing*.

R. Socher, E.H. Huang, J. Pennington, C.D. Manning, and A.Y. Ng. 2011a. Dynamic pooling and unfolding recursive autoencoders for paraphrase detection. In *Proc. NIPS*.

R. Socher, J. Pennington, E.H. Huang, A.Y. Ng, and C.D. Manning. 2011b. Semi-supervised recursive autoencoders for predicting sentiment distributions. In *Proc. EMNLP*.

R. Socher, B. Huval, C.D. Manning, and A.Y. Ng. 2012. Semantic compositionality through recursive matrix-vector spaces. In *Proc. EMNLP*.

R. Socher, A. Perelygin, J. Wu, J. Chuang, C.D. Manning, A.Y. Ng, and C. Potts. 2013. Recursive deep models for semantic compositionality over a sentiment treebank. In *Proc. EMNLP*.

R. Socher, A. Karpathy, Q.V. Le, C.D. Manning, and A.Y. Ng. 2014. Grounded compositional semantics for finding and describing images with sentences. *TACL*.

N. Srivastava, G. Hinton, A. Krizhevsky, I. Sutskever, and R. Salakhutdinov. 2014. Dropout: A simple way to prevent neural networks from overfitting. *JMLR*, 15(1).

K.S. Tai, R. Socher, and C.D. Manning. 2015. Improved semantic representations from tree-structured long short-term memory networks. In *Proc. ACL*.

D.H.D. Warren and F.C.N. Pereira. 1982. An efficient easily adaptable system for interpreting natural language queries. *American Journal of Computational Linguistics*.

Y. Watanabe, J. Mizuno, E. Nichols, N. Okazaki, and K. Inui. 2012. A latent discriminative model for compositional entailment relation recognition using natural logic. In *Proc. COLING*.

M.D. Zeiler. 2012. ADADELTA: An adaptive learning rate method. arXiv:1212.5701.

J.M. Zelle and R.J. Mooney. 1996. Learning to parse database queries using inductive logic programming. In *Proc. AAAI*.

L.S. Zettlemoyer and M. Collins. 2005. Learning to map sentences to logical form: Structured classification with probabilistic categorial grammars. In *Proc. of the 21st Conference on Uncertainty in Artificial Intelligence*.

Concept Extensions as the Basis for Vector-Space Semantics: Combining Distributional and Ontological Information about Entities

Jackie Chi Kit Cheung
McGill University
3480 University
Montreal, Quebec, Canada
jcheung@cs.mcgill.ca

Abstract

We propose to base the development of vector-space models of semantics on concept extensions, which defines concepts to be sets of entities. We investigate two sources of knowledge about entities that could be relevant: distributional information provided by word or phrase embeddings, and ontological information derived from a knowledge base. We develop a feedforward neural network architecture to learn entity representations that are used to predict their concept memberships, and show that the two sources of information are actually complementary. In an entity ranking experiment, the combination approach that uses both types of information outperforms models that only rely on one of the two. We also perform an analysis of the output using fuzzy logic techniques to demonstrate the potential of learning concept extensions for supporting inference involving classical semantic operations.

1 Introduction

The *extensional definition*, or *denotation*, of a concept is the set of entities in the world to which that concept applies. For example, the definition of *Celebrity* would be the set of entities in the world, including *Will Smith*, *Paris Hilton*, etc.

In formal semantics and pragmatics, this conception of meaning has played an important role in the accounts of a wide range of compositional constructions, including definite and indefinite articles, quantifiers, presuppositions, and intersective adjectives. For example, the extension of a noun phrase such as *"red apple"* that is composed of a noun and a modifying adjective is derived by taking the set intersection of the extensions of *"red"* and *"apple"*. In an applied setting, explicitly enumerating the members of these extensions seems to be an impossible task, as there are large numbers of entities and relations, not to mention infinitely many possible contexts and domains. Thus, the direct application of this view of semantics would seem to be confined to limited domains.

Distributional semantics is a potential solution to this problem. The long-touted advantages of distributional approaches are that they can be easily trained from a large corpus, and they enable a graded notion of similarity. Typically, such models are trained to optimize distributional criteria based on similarity correlations or predicting a word in context. However, it is not enough to rely solely on these criteria. Similarity only supports *relative* reasoning about relations between concepts, and it is difficult to adapt such measures to make *absolute* inferences about the truth value of a proposition. The applications of distributional semantics (DS) to date have reflected this bias. The most common approach to evaluate DS models has been to correlate predicted similarity judgments against judgments gathered from humans (Finkelstein et al., 2002; Agirre et al., 2012). More recent applications in paraphrase detection (Socher et al., 2011), textual entailment (Beltagy et al., 2013) and analogical reasoning (Mikolov et al., 2013) are also primarily concerned with the relationships between phrases.

A more serious issue is that distributional semantics alone seems to be insufficient for handling rarely occurring events and entities, if we treat them as just another target phrase in the corpus. Consider the following passage:

Proceedings of the 3rd Workshop on Continuous Vector Space Models and their Compositionality (CVSC), pages 22–31,
Beijing, China, July 26-31, 2015.

(1) *He is an American actor, producer, and rapper. As of 2014, 17 of the 21 films in which he has had leading roles have accumulated worldwide gross earnings of over $100 million each.*

Given just this short description of the entity, we are able to make several inferences about its properties. For example, we are able to infer that this entity is a male human, working in the entertainment industry. He can most likely vote in American elections, obtain a passport, and he is likely a wealthy celebrity, given the success of the movies he has acted in. We might even be able to guess the identity of this person (Will Smith)[1].

While it may be possible to learn these characteristics from the contexts of the bigram *"Will Smith"* in a large training corpus, this is less plausible for a rarely occurring, or perhaps an entirely invented entity. Clearly, these inferences are enabled by extracting the concept and relational information present in the local context, then relating them to other concepts of interest based on our knowledge of the world.

In this paper, we propose to use concept extension predictions as the overall training objective of a vector-space model of semantics. While distributional information will still be a crucial component of our model, what distinguishes our approach is that it optimizes directly for an objective which is well justified by compositional theories of semantics, rather than an objective that is internal to considerations within distributional semantics such as similarity measurements.

To predict these concept extensions, we train a model that learns a representation of an input entity using features derived from distributional semantics and ontological information derived from a knowledge base. Our model, which we call *Ontological Distributional Semantics*, employs a simple feedforward neural network architecture to learn interactions between these two sources of information.

We conduct experiments on Freebase (Bollacker et al., 2008), taking Freebase types to be concepts, and the entity set that the Freebase type contains to be that concept's extension. The results of an entity ranking experiment show that Ontological Distributed Semantics outperforms either distributed representations or ontological information alone across three entity classes.

[1]This passage is an edited version of his Wikipedia article.

Because a large, complete knowledge base may not always be available, we further test our model under conditions in which there is incomplete ontological knowledge about an entity, and we analyze the relative contributions of the distributional and ontological components of our model.

Finally, to illustrate how our approach can take advantage of insights from classical approaches to semantics, we develop a method to extract semantic relations between concepts from the output predictions of our model without further training using fuzzy set logic operations. These results argue for the importance of learning concept extensions not just to develop a better model of entities, but also as a potential method to better integrate distributional semantics with formal, compositional approaches to semantics.

2 Related Work

Several models have recently been proposed which combine distributional with ontological information (Fried and Duh, 2014; Yang et al., 2014). The goal of these papers is to encode the ontological relationships as some kind of regularity in the learned vector space, usually as a linear transformation; e.g., that objective encourages there to be a consistent vector addition operation that represents the part-of relationship between two concepts. By contrast, our work argues for an entirely different kind of objective function for a vector-space model motivated by classical compositional semantics.

Herbelot and Ganesalingam (2013) investigate KL-divergence of a semantic vector as a simple information-theoretic measure to determine hypernym/hyponym relations, but found that this was outperformed by a word frequency baseline. Other work employs distributional similarity to learn to cluster concepts into a hierarchy (Yamada et al., 2009, for example). There have also been supervised methods for hypernymy detection (Roller et al., 2014, for example). Typically, this is done for upward-entailing concept-to-concept reasoning, for example between word pairs (e.g., *van* entails *car*) as in the BLESS data set (Baroni and Lenci, 2011).

Another thread of related work is in relation extraction (Banko et al., 2007; Bunescu and Mooney, 2007; Riedel et al., 2013, for example), and knowledge base population, such as the TAC shared task (McNamee and Dang, 2009). This work is concerned with extracting the relationships between entities, in order to improve the quality of a database. Our work can be seen as a way of integrating distributional semantics into large-scale reasoning about entities.

Most recently, Gupta et al. (2015) investigate a similar problem, using a logistic regression model to map features derived from distributional methods to referential properties of countries that are derived from Freebase. In our work, we explore the effect of combining distributional and ontological information, and perform a number of analyses on the output of our models.

3 Framework and Model

Our model is designed to learn entity representations that are useful for predicting concept extensions, which are sets of entities in the domain. Let $C = \{c_1, c_2, ...\}$ be the set of concepts of interest, and $E = \{e_1, e_2, ...\}$ be the set of entities. Since we are interested in extensional meaning, each concept c is defined by its extension, *exten*(c), a set of elements drawn from E. Rather than explicitly enumerating these sets, we instead aim to learn a function $f : E \rightarrow \mathcal{P}(C)$ that maps an input entity to the concepts of which it is an element. For example, $f($*Will Smith*$)$ would evaluate to the concepts *Male* and *Actor*, but also $\neg$*Female*, among others.

We frame this as a supervised multi-label classification problem. For an entity $e \in E$, the input to the classifier is a feature vector representation of the entity, $\vec{x}$. The classifier predicts a binary output vector $\vec{y}$ of length $|C|$, in which $y_k = 1$ means that $e \in$ *exten*(c_k), and $y_k = 0$ means that $e \notin$ *exten*(c_k). In our experiments, we will actually assume that the classifier makes probabilistic, "soft" decisions, so that the entries of the output vector will range from 0 to 1, representing the predicted probability of the entity being a member of the concept extension.

It is possible to view this task as a series of standard binary classification problems, one for each of the concepts. However, this would require training a large number of concept-specific models. Our hope in learning entity representations is that they will be more generally useful, for example, in a compositional setting in which inferences are to be made about phrases containing entities for which we have already learned a representation.

3.1 Input features

We now specify the input feature vector representation of the entity, as well as a learning algorithm for the function f. Our full model combines ontological information with pre-trained distributional semantic vectors to learn the extensional meaning of concepts. To measure the effect of each of these components, we also train baseline versions of the model that omit one or the other feature set. Thus, we compare the following three sets of features:

DS We derive a *distributional vector* of features from word2vec, a popular recent approach to distributional semantics (Mikolov et al., 2013). We use the 300-dimensional pre-trained vectors available on their website, which include both single-word and multi-word entities. We chose word2vec as it is a popular recent model of distributional semantics which has been shown to work well on a variety of existing semantic tasks (Baroni et al., 2014). We leave the comparison of this model to other recent distributional semantic models (Pennington et al., 2014, for example) to future work.

ONTO For the ontological features, we derive an *ontological vector* of an entity from its Freebase entry. Each dimension of the ontological vector corresponds to a concept, represented by a Freebase type. The vector takes a value of 1 at that dimension if the entity is an instance of that concept, and 0 otherwise. For example, if the first three dimensions of the ontological vector correspond to the concepts *Male*, *Actor*, and *Female*, their values for the ontological vector of *Will Smith* would be 1, 1, and 0, respectively.

ONTODS We concatenate the above two feature vectors into an ontological distributional semantic vector.

3.2 Learning algorithm

The learning algorithm of our model is a simple feedforward neural network. The neural network has one hidden layer, the entity representation, which is then used to predict the output vector $\vec{y}$. The network is trained by stochastic gradient descent with a mean squared error loss, a sigmoid nonlinearity and weight decay. All of the parameters to the model are tuned according to performance on a held-out development set (Section 4.1).

Using a neural network offers several advantages. First, despite its simplicity, it is able to learn

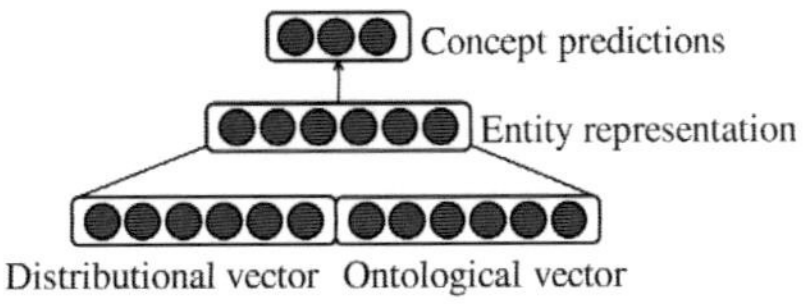

Figure 1: Graphical representation of the ONTODS model as a feedforward neural network architecture

a more complex function over the vector space than the typical candidates for inference with distributional semantics; namely, vector addition and cosine similarity. Second, we are able to train one model that jointly predicts all of the concept labels in one feedforward pass, rather than training separate classifiers for each concept. A graphical representation of the architecture of our model is presented in Figure 1.

Note that in this architecture, both the ontological features in the input vector and the predictions in the output vector refer to the membership of the entity in concept extensions. In our experiments, the features in the output vector will actually be a subset of the features in the ontological vector, because we will only use the model to make predictions about the most commonly occurring concepts. This design architecture is reminiscent of autoencoders, which have been applied to learn a compositionality function for distributional semantics (Socher et al., 2011), though in our case, the input and output vectors are not identical. Our use of regularization, weight decay, and parameter tuning on a development set prevents the model from overfitting to the training data by simply mirroring the appropriate values of the input vector.

4 Experiments

Our experiments were conducted on the collaborative knowledge base, Freebase. We extracted three classes of entities from the June 9, 2014 dump of Freebase by taking instances of top-level concepts (i.e., Freebase types) corresponding to People, Organizations, and Locations, as shown in Table 1. We chose these classes because they are the entity classes most often modelled by other work in NLP, such as by NER taggers (Finkel et al., 2005). These classes also tend to be a part of many different scenarios, thus there should be rich ontological structures to learn. In addition to the entities, we extracted all of the concepts that these entities are tagged with, in order to construct the ontological vector component of our model.

We then filtered the entities and concepts according to several frequency and quality criteria. For entities, we required the following characteristics: *(1)* there must be a word2vec vector available for that entity, as determined by a string match to the entity's name or one of its aliases; *(2)* the entity must belong to a minimum of five concepts; *(3)* the entity must satisfy a minimum frequency threshold, as follows.

We estimate the frequency of an entity by taking the frequency of the name of the entity in the Gigaword corpus. Where the name consists of multiple words, the minimum of these is taken. We used a frequency threshold of 150, which is actually quite low given the size of the Gigaword corpus. We chose to filter on frequency so that the distributional component would have seen the entity often enough to learn something useful about it.

Of the roughly one million entities in Freebase in these three categories, 84,286 entities passed the above filters.

For the concepts, we required the following characteristics: *(1)* the concept must contain a minimum of ten entity instances; *(2)* the concept must not be a /user or /m type. The second criterion removes many concepts that are overly specific and only of interest to a particular user, containing for example lists of landmarks that a user would like to visit. In addition, we removed the concept used to construct an entity category, and the concept /common/topic, because all of the entities in an entity class would be instances of these concepts. 1,262 concepts of the original 5,024 were retained after filtering.

Following filtering, the remaining entities are randomly assigned to training, development, and test sets in a 60%-20%-20% split. Table 1 provides a summary of several statistics about the data sets that we extracted.

4.1 Method

We applied the models described above to predict the concept memberships of entities in the fifty most common concepts of each entity class. We focused on the most common concepts, because they are likely to be the important high-level divisions in the entity class, and are also more likely

Entity category	**Freebase ID**	***N* entities** (train + dev + test)	***N* concepts**
People	/people/person	23053 + 7684 + 7685	530
Organizations	/organization/organization	4771 + 1591 + 1591	260
Locations	/location/location	22746 + 7582 + 7583	472

Table 1: Basic statistics concerning the subsets of Freebase that we extracted for our experiments. **Freebase ID** refers to the top-level concept used to define the entity classes that we extract. ***N*** represents the count of unique entities or concepts.

to be correctly annotated. These fifty concepts to be predicted are themselves part of the ontological vector used in the ONTO and ONTODS models. To ensure that the models do not have access to the label to be predicted at prediction time, we predict the membership for each concept separately, and mask the corresponding element of the ontological vector by setting it to zero. So, if we are predicting whether an entity is *Male*, we set the dimension corresponding to the *Male* concept in the input ontological vector to 0. We repeat this process for each concept to be predicted in the output vector. In Section 4.3, we will also test the effect of having only partial or no ontological information in the ontological vector for the ONTO and ONTODS models.

We train the feedforward neural network model by backpropagation using stochastic gradient descent with a decreasing learning rate schedule, and weight decay to prevent overfitting. To tune the parameters involved, as well as other parameters such as the number of units in the hidden layer, the amount of randomness in the initialization of the weight matrices, and the number of training epochs to perform, we use the Spearmint Bayesian optimization package (Snoek et al., 2012). We tune the parameters on the held-out development set for each entity class separately. For almost all of the models, training for 20 iterations with 100 hidden units achieves the best performance on the development set [2].

As our evaluation measure, we adopt mean average precision (MAP) from work in relation extraction and information retrieval. For each concept, the predictions from the model results in a ranking of entities that belong to the concept, in decreasing order of probability. This ranking is compared against the gold-standard extracted from FreeBase using the average precision measure:

$$AP = \frac{\sum_{k=1}^{N}(P(k) \times rel(k))}{N}, \quad (2)$$

where $P(k)$ is the precision of the top k entities ranked by our model, $rel(k)$ is an indicator function that is 1 exactly when the kth entity is correctly predicted to be an instance of the concept, and N is the total number of entities that this concept contains. The mean average precision (MAP) is then the mean of the average precisions over all concepts. MAP is the appropriate measure for this task, as classification accuracy would give a misleading picture of performance; most entities do not belong to most concepts, so simply predicting that all entities belong to no concepts would give a very high accuracy score.

[2] The best parameter settings are available on the author's website or upon request.

	People	**Organ.**	**Loc.**
DS	45.06	43.66	38.15
ONTO	41.12	47.55	73.26
ONTODS	**50.04**	**56.60**	**75.63**

Table 2: Entity ranking results by input feature set in terms of the mean average precision measure (%). All differences are statistically significant by a randomized bootstrap test at $p < 0.0001$.

4.2 Results

The results of our concept prediction models are presented in Table 2. All differences in MAP between models trained on the same data set are statistically significant, by the randomized bootstrap method. The results show that our ONTODS model achieves the best performance on all three entity classes in terms of MAP, outperforming both the ONTO and the DS models. Comparing ONTO and DS, DS achieves better performance on People, but not on Organization, and is substantially worse on Locations.

People	Organizations	Locations
/people/deceased_person	/dining/restaurant	/architecture/venue
Benjamin Franklin 1	Cold Stone Creamery 1	Staples Center 1
Christopher Columbus 1	Rainforest Cafe 1	Candlestick Park 1
Ronald Reagan 1	Frontera Grill 1	MTS Centre 1
Duke Ellington 1	Waffle House 1	Xcel Energy Center 1
/film/music_contributor	/organization/organization_member	/geography/river
Frank Sinatra 0	MIT 1	Yamuna 1
Sean Combs 0	University of Virginia 1	Sugar Creek 1
Fred Astaire 0	University of Connecticut 0	Sugar Creek 1
Ice Cube 1	DirecTV Group 0	Brazos River 1

Figure 2: The highest-ranked entities for six select concepts according to the ONTODS model. Next to the name of the entity, a 1 indicates that the entity belongs to the concept according to Freebase, and 0 means it does not. For the river concept, Sugar Creek appears twice due to a duplicate entry in Freebase.

model: condition	People	Organ.	Loc.
ONTO: half	29.62	32.76	58.28
ONTO: all-but-one	41.12	47.55	73.26
ONTODS: none	32.62	40.42	27.08
ONTODS: half	44.85	48.78	65.08
ONTODS: all-but-one	**50.04**	**56.60**	**75.63**

Table 3: Entity ranking results in the partial ontological information experiment, by MAP (%). The results from "all-but-one" rows are identical to corresponding rows in Table 2.

Figure 2 shows several rankings made by the best performing ONTODS model for different concepts. Overall, almost all of the top rankings are correct according to the information extracted from Freebase. Several apparently incorrect rankings seem to be related to problems with the coverage of Freebase. For example, Frank Sinatra, Sean Combs, and Fred Astaire are not labelled as film music contributors in the version of Freebase we used. Other errors are in categories that seem to be less well-defined, such as /organization/organization_member, a concept that describes entities that belong to some other unspecified organization.

4.3 Partial Ontological Information

Earlier, we motivated the need for ontological information to model rare occurring or invented entities, yet knowledge bases are incomplete, and reliable ontological information about an entity is not always available. In this section, we simulate having partial ontological information of an input entity by masking some of the features in the ontological vector. In future work, we would like to design a system that can extract ontological information about an entity from a short passage.

Using the same trained models from the previous section, we conducted experiments in which we mask some of the input features in the ontological vector under the following three conditions, representing a decreasing amount of available information about an entity:

All-but-one This condition represents the same setting as the previous experiments, in which the model predicts the output features one at a time, and has access to all of the ontological features except for the one being predicted.

Half We ranked the output concepts by the number of entities that they contain, and then assigned them into two groups in an alternating manner. The two groups of concepts are thus roughly matched in terms of the number of entities they contain. We predict each group separately, masking those concepts in the input ontological vector; i.e., when predicting the first group of concepts, the model only has access to information about the second group of concepts, and vice versa.

None We masked all of the concepts to be predicted in the ontological vector, setting all of those features to zero. Note that the model still has access to the remaining ontological features that are not in the output vector. Thus, this setting still has access to some ontological information, unlike the DS model.

	Avg. Max. Jaccard
People	0.3525
Organizations	0.4509
Locations	0.5717

Table 4: Average maximum Jaccard similarity for the top 50 concepts in each entity class

We applied the ONTODS model under all of these conditions, and the ONTO model under the all-but-one and half conditions only, as we found that it would have very little information to make predictions on under the none condition. We used the same best performing models from the previous experiment, as the training was not affected. The results of this experiment are presented in Table 3. Unsurprisingly, the performance of both models degrade substantially when given only partial ontological information. Note, however, that the ONTODS model in the half condition is still better than the DS and ONTO models in the all-but-one condition on two of the three entity classes.

4.4 Discussions

What accounts for the differing contributions of the ontological and the distributional components to the performance for the different entity classes? In particular, ontological information seems to be especially important for the Locations entity class, whereas distributional information seems to be better for the People entity class. We consider the correlations between the different concepts as an explanation for this result. Intuitively, the greater the correlations between the concepts for a certain entity class, the more useful ontological information is in making inferences about concept memberships of entities.

We compute a measure based on Jaccard similarity between the concepts for this analysis. For each of the top 50 concepts represented in the output vector, we find the maximum Jaccard similarity between that concept and the other concepts in the training set:

$$maxJ(c) = \max_{c'} \frac{|exten(c) \cap exten(c')|}{|exten(c) \cup exten(c')|}. \quad (3)$$

Then, we take the average of this maximum Jaccard similarity over the top 50 concepts. We use the maximum similarity to other concepts rather than the average; the average similarity could be low due to having many unrelated concepts, which a statistical learner would identify as irrelevant. Across the three entity classes, the ranking of the average maximum Jaccard similarity matches the apparent importance of the ontological component of the models in the entity ranking task (Table 4). This result provides an explanation for the different performances of the models in the entity ranking task, and could be used to approximate model performance given a new data set.

5 Deriving Semantic Relations

We further analyze our model's performance by examining its ability to recognize semantic relations between concepts. This analysis is not a formal evaluation of the models, but serves two purposes. First, it is a qualitative test of the entity rankings of our model. Second, it demonstrates inferences that follow directly from concept extension predictions without the need to train yet another special-purpose classifier, for example to determine hypernymy or synonymy.

Whereas relations such as hypernymy and synonymy follow directly from crisp, 0-1 concept extensions predictions, we choose instead to use the ranking probabilities that are the output of our model. This avoids issues with choosing an appropriate cut-off for the predictions, and also allows the models to make soft predictions of lexical semantic relations between concepts. We focus below on hypernym/hyponym relations; because Freebase explicitly attempts to standardize and canonicalize all entities and types, we do not expect to find good synonyms.

We thus view the predictions produced by the models as fuzzy sets (Zadeh, 1965)[3], and use standard operations from fuzzy set logic to determine hypernymy. Our models above learn a function $\vec{y} = f(\vec{x})$, where y_k is the probability that the input entity belongs to concept c_k. For a given concept c_k, let us now aggregate the model predictions over all entities into a vector $\mu_k(x)$, which has a length equal to the number of entities in the data set. This can be seen as a membership function of a fuzzy set that provides a score between 0 and 1 of an entity x in $exten(c_k)$. We use the follow-

[3]We leave aside the philosophical issue of whether our models' output values should be interpreted as probabilities of set membership or degrees of set membership.

c_i	c_j	$\subseteq$	$\supseteq$	c_i	c_j	$\subseteq$	$\supseteq$
People ONTODS				**People** DS			
tv_program_guest	/film/actor	0.99	0.35	cricket_bowler	cricket_player	0.99	0.68
theater_actor	/film/actor	0.99	0.41	olympic_athlete	pro_athlete	0.98	0.18
celebrity	/film/actor	0.95	0.43	football_player	pro_athlete	0.97	0.18
Organizations ONTODS				**Organizations** DS			
venture_company	employer	1.0	0.08	airline	employer	0.99	0.03
football_team	sports_team	0.99	0.22	airline	aircraft_owner	0.98	0.91
restaurant	employer	0.99	0.05	university	educ_inst	0.92	0.85
Locations ONTODS				**Locations** DS			
river	geog_feature	0.99	0.28	capital_admin_div	stat_region	0.99	0.09
river	body_of_water	0.97	0.38	university	educ_inst	0.95	0.91
body_of_water	geog_feature	0.97	0.70	building	structure	0.96	0.57

Figure 3: Scores for several subset and superset relations learned by two of our models using fuzzy set logic operations. The $\subseteq$ columns display the score *hypo*(c_i, c_j), while the $\supseteq$ columns display *hypo*(c_j, c_i). We have abbreviated several concept names for space reasons.

ing definitions of intersection and union between fuzzy sets A and B:

$$\mu_{A \cap B} = \min(\mu_A, \mu_B) \quad (4)$$

$$\mu_{A \cup B} = \max(\mu_A, \mu_B). \quad (5)$$

A concept c is a hyponymy of another concept c' if $exten(c) \subseteq exten(c')$. We determine the subset relation in fuzzy logic reducing it to fuzzy set intersection and set equality, and we determine fuzzy set equality by using a generalized version of Jaccard similarity using L1-norms:

$$A \subset B \leftrightarrow A \cap B = A \quad (6)$$

$$fuzzyJ(\mu_A, \mu_B) = \frac{\|\mu_{A \cap B}\|_1}{\|\mu_{A \cup B}\|_1}. \quad (7)$$

The degree of hyponymy of c_i to c_j, *hypo*(c_i, c_j), is then simply *hypo*$(c_i, c_j) =$ *fuzzyJ*$(\mu_{i \cap j}, \mu_i)$.

We present several subset relations discovered by the ONTODS and DS models in Figure 3, as indicated by a high *hypo* score between the concepts. We chose these models because the former is the best-performing model in entity ranking, and the latter does not include ontological information in its entity representation. This method finds several good hyponym/hypernym relations, such as football_team $\subseteq$ sports_team, and restaurant $\subseteq$ employer. It also finds chains of relations, such as sports_facility $\subseteq$ venue $\subseteq$ structure, and river $\subseteq$ body_of_water $\subseteq$ geographical_feature.

6 Conclusion

We have argued that concept extensions can form the basis of a vector-space model of semantics. Our model learns entity representations by combining ontological information derived from a knowledge base with distributional information trained to predict concept extensions. Our experiments indicate the success of this model, and we perform several analyses to explain the relative importance of the ontological and distributional semantic components of our model, as well as the ability of the model to recover semantic relations between concepts using fuzzy set logic.

Learning concept extensions provides a method to integrate distributional semantics with formal, compositional semantics. For example, semantic relations between concepts could be detected based on their formal, set-theoretic definitions, as shown in Section 5. The framework and model presented in this paper suggest a natural way to predict these and other semantic relations without the need for another classification step.

It would also be interesting to see whether the ontological information/concept extensions, which in this work was supplied by a knowledge base, could be derived or augmented through other means, such as by using image data (Young et al., 2014).

Acknowledgments

We would like to thank Patricia Araujo Thaine, Aida Nematzadeh, Nissan Pow, and the anonymous reviewers for useful discussions and feedback. This work is funded by the Natural Sciences and Engineering Research Council of Canada.

References

Eneko Agirre, Mona Diab, Daniel Cer, and Aitor Gonzalez-Agirre. 2012. Semeval-2012 task 6: A pilot on semantic textual similarity. In *Proceedings of the First Joint Conference on Lexical and Computational Semantics-Volume 1: Proceedings of the main conference and the shared task, and Volume 2: Proceedings of the Sixth International Workshop on Semantic Evaluation*, pages 385–393. Association for Computational Linguistics.

Michele Banko, Michael J. Cafarella, Stephen Soderland, Matthew Broadhead, and Oren Etzioni. 2007. Open information extraction for the web. In *IJCAI*, volume 7, pages 2670–2676.

Marco Baroni and Alessandro Lenci. 2011. How we BLESSed distributional semantic evaluation. In *Proceedings of the GEMS 2011 Workshop on GEometrical Models of Natural Language Semantics*, pages 1–10. Association for Computational Linguistics.

Marco Baroni, Georgiana Dinu, and Germán Kruszewski. 2014. Don't count, predict! a systematic comparison of context-counting vs. context-predicting semantic vectors. In *Proceedings of the 52nd Annual Meeting of the Association for Computational Linguistics (Volume 1: Long Papers)*, pages 238–247, Baltimore, Maryland, June. Association for Computational Linguistics.

Islam Beltagy, Cuong Chau, Gemma Boleda, Dan Garrette, Katrin Erk, and Raymond Mooney. 2013. Montague meets Markov: Deep semantics with probabilistic logical form. In *Proceedings of the Second Joint Conference on Lexical and Computational Semantics (*SEM-2013)*.

Kurt Bollacker, Colin Evans, Praveen Paritosh, Tim Sturge, and Jamie Taylor. 2008. Freebase: a collaboratively created graph database for structuring human knowledge. In *Proceedings of the 2008 ACM SIGMOD international conference on Management of data*, pages 1247–1250. ACM.

Razvan C. Bunescu and Raymond J. Mooney. 2007. Learning to extract relations from the web using minimal supervision. In *Proceedings of the 45th Annual Meeting of the Association for Computational Linguistics*, volume 45, pages 576–583.

Jenny R. Finkel, Trond Grenager, and Christopher Manning. 2005. Incorporating non-local information into information extraction systems by Gibbs sampling. In *Proceedings of the 43rd Annual Meeting of the Association for Computational Linguistics (ACL'05)*, pages 363–370, Ann Arbor, Michigan, June. Association for Computational Linguistics.

Lev Finkelstein, Evgeniy Gabrilovich, Yossi Matias, Ehud Rivlin, Zach Solan, Gadi Wolfman, and Eytan Ruppin. 2002. Placing search in context: The concept revisited. *ACM Transactions on Information Systems*, 20(1):116–131.

Daniel Fried and Kevin Duh. 2014. Incorporating both distributional and relational semantics in word representations. *arXiv preprint arXiv:1412.4369*.

Abhijeet Gupta, Gemma Boleda, Marco Baroni, and Sebastian Padó. 2015. Mapping conceptual features to referential properties. In *Proceedings of the 3rd International ESSENCE Workshop: Algorithms for Processing Meaning*.

Aurélie Herbelot and Mohan Ganesalingam. 2013. Measuring semantic content in distributional vectors. In *Proceedings of the 51st Annual Meeting of the Association for Computational Linguistics (Volume 2: Short Papers)*, pages 440–445, Sofia, Bulgaria, August. Association for Computational Linguistics.

Paul McNamee and Hoa T. Dang. 2009. Overview of the TAC 2009 knowledge base population track. In *Text Analysis Conference (TAC)*, volume 17, pages 111–113.

Tomas Mikolov, Wen-tau Yih, and Geoffrey Zweig. 2013. Linguistic regularities in continuous space word representations. In *Proceedings of the 2013 Conference of the North American Chapter of the Association for Computational Linguistics: Human Language Technologies*, pages 746–751, Atlanta, Georgia, June. Association for Computational Linguistics.

Jeffrey Pennington, Richard Socher, and Christopher Manning. 2014. Glove: Global vectors for word representation. In *Proceedings of the 2014 Conference on Empirical Methods in Natural Language Processing (EMNLP)*, pages 1532–1543, Doha, Qatar, October. Association for Computational Linguistics.

Sebastian Riedel, Limin Yao, Andrew McCallum, and Benjamin M. Marlin. 2013. Relation extraction with matrix factorization and universal schemas. In *Proceedings of the 2013 Conference of the North American Chapter of the Association for Computational Linguistics: Human Language Technologies*, pages 74–84, Atlanta, Georgia, June. Association for Computational Linguistics.

Stephen Roller, Katrin Erk, and Gemma Boleda. 2014. Inclusive yet selective: Supervised distributional hypernymy detection. In *Proceedings of COLING 2014, the 25th International Conference on Computational Linguistics: Technical Papers*, pages 1025–1036, Dublin, Ireland, August. Dublin City University and Association for Computational Linguistics.

Jasper Snoek, Hugo Larochelle, and Ryan P. Adams. 2012. Practical bayesian optimization of machine learning algorithms. In *Advances in Neural Information Processing Systems*, pages 2951–2959.

Richard Socher, Eric H. Huang, Jeffrey Pennin, Christopher D. Manning, and Andrew Ng. 2011. Dynamic pooling and unfolding recursive autoencoders for paraphrase detection. In *Advances in Neural Information Processing Systems*, pages 801–809.

Ichiro Yamada, Kentaro Torisawa, Jun'ichi Kazama, Kow Kuroda, Masaki Murata, Stijn De Saeger, Francis Bond, and Asuka Sumida. 2009. Hypernym discovery based on distributional similarity and hierarchical structures. In *Proceedings of the 2009 Conference on Empirical Methods in Natural Language Processing*, pages 929–937, Singapore, August. Association for Computational Linguistics.

Bishan Yang, Wen-tau Yih, Xiaodong He, Jianfeng Gao, and Li Deng. 2014. Embedding entities and relations for learning and inference in knowledge bases. *arXiv preprint arXiv:1412.6575*.

Peter Young, Alice Lai, Micah Hodosh, and Julia Hockenmaier. 2014. From image descriptions to visual denotations: New similarity metrics for semantic inference over event descriptions. *Transactions of the Association for Computational Linguistics*, 2:67–78.

Lotfi A. Zadeh. 1965. Fuzzy sets. *Information and Control*, 8(3):338–353.

Joint Semantic Relevance Learning with Text Data and Graph Knowledge

Dongxu Zhang[1,3], **Bin Yuan**[1,3], **Dong Wang**[*1,2], **Rong Liu**[1,4]
[1]CSLT, RIIT, Tsinghua University
[2]Tsinghua National Lab for Information Science and Technology
[3]PRIS, Beijing University of Posts and Telecommunications
[4]Huilan Limited, Beijing, P.R. China
{zhangdx,yuanb,lr}@cslt.riit.tsinghua.edu.cn
wangdong99@mails.tsinghua.edu.cn

Abstract

Inferring semantic relevance among entities (e.g., entries of Wikipedia) is important and challenging. According to the information resources, the inference can be categorized into learning with either raw text data, or labeled text data (e.g., wiki page), or graph knowledge (e.g, WordNet). Although graph knowledge tends to be more reliable, text data is much less costly and offers a better coverage.

We show in this paper that different resources are complementary and can be combined to improve semantic learning. Particularly, we present a joint learning approach that learns vectors of entities by leveraging resources of both text data and graph knowledge. The experiments conducted on the semantic relatedness task show that text-based learning works well on general domain tasks, however for tasks in specific domains, joint learning that involves both text data and graph knowledge offers significant improvement.

1 Introduction

With the development of deep learning and the establishment of large knowledge bases, knowledge embedding has gained much interest in natural language processing. In general, knowledge can be represented by some *entities* that represent semantic concepts, plus the *relations* among them. Knowledge embedding involves representing entities of knowledge bases in a low-dimensional continuous space so that the relations among them can be well represented. The embedding can be conducted with different objectives with different tasks in concern. This paper focuses on the semantic learning task which intends to optimize the semantic relevance among entities by knowledge embedding, e.g., inferring appropriate knowledge (entity) vectors.

According to the information resource that is used to learn with, knowledge embedding can be classified into three categories: raw text learning, labeled text learning and graph knowledge learning. In the raw text learning, the entities are treated as words or phrases, and the local word context information in the raw text is used to drive the embedding. Various approaches of word/phrase embedding belong to this category (Huang et al., 2012; Mikolov et al., 2013). In the labeled text learning, the embedding is based on the description text associated to each entity. A simple approach belonging to this category derives the vector of an entity by averaging the word vectors of the description associated to the entity. Essentially, the knowledge used in this learning is the co-occurrence statistics of the words in the descriptions. Finally, in the graph knowledge learning, the relations among entities labeled by people are used to direct the embedding. Representative approaches of this category include TransE (Bordes et al., 2013) and NTN (Socher et al., 2013).

Different information resources possess their respective advantages and disadvantages. Raw text is totally unstructured and unsupervised (no data annotated). The training data is easy to be collected and in most cases, it offers good entity coverage. The shortcoming, however, is that the useful information is often buried in noise and therefore it is not trivial to extract the desired information. Finally, the learning purely relies on word occurrence statistics, which often under-estimates entities that are infrequent in the training data.

labeled text offers a text description for each entity, so it is more supervised than raw text in the sense that some human-specified annotations are involved. However, the supervision is rather weak, since the relations among entities are not explicitly annotated but implicitly encoded within word co-occurrences of entity descriptions. A particular advantage of the labeled text learning is that the entities that are difficult to learn with raw text because of their limited occurrences can be learned

Proceedings of the 3rd Workshop on Continuous Vector Space Models and their Compositionality (CVSC), pages 32–40,
Beijing, China, July 26-31, 2015.

by referring to the words in the descriptions, for instance by averaging the vectors of the words.

Finally, graph knowledge is the most structured and supervised information resource. It is annotated by people and therefore is much more clean and reliable, and the relations among entities can be far beyond the ones that are represented by word local contexts as in raw text. Additionally, the learning does not rely on word statistics and so is mostly suitable for new and infrequent entities, for instance those in a specific domain. An obvious disadvantage of graph knowledge is the high cost in data annotation and the low coverage of the entities and relations. The emergence of large-scale public knowledge bases such as Freebase and Yago partly solved the problem, however for many infrequent entities, the annotations are far from satisfactory and most of the relations are missing.

Due to the respective advantages and disadvantages of different information resources, it is natural to combine them to provide better knowledge embedding. A number of researches have been conducted in this direction. For example, Yu and Dredze (2014) proposed a method to employ graph knowledge to improve word embedding, and Weston et al. (2013) used text data to assist new relation discovery for graph knowledge bases. Nevertheless, there is not a satisfactory framework to learn with multiple and heterogeneous information resources. Particularly, there is limited investigation on to what extent heterogeneous information can be complementary and how they contribute in different situations.

This paper presents a joint learning approach that learns entity vectors by leveraging resources of both raw and labeled text as well as graph knowledge. We first present a joint text learning approach which learns word and entity vectors together with both raw and labeled text. This is similar to the paragraph vector (PV) model (Le and Mikolov, 2014) though a different training approach is adopted in our study. This joint text learning approach is then combined with the graph knowledge learning to form a joint text and graph learning, by integrating the cost functions of the two learning methods.

The experiments are conducted with three information resources: Wikipedia as the raw and labeled text, WordNet and Yago as the graph knowledge. The entity relatedness task is selected to evaluate the performance of the learning methods. Two scenarios have been conducted, one is based on WordNet and the other is based on Yago. The test on WordNet is a general domain task while the test on Yago is a specific domain task. The experimental results show that the joint text learning offers consistent improvement compared to learning with raw text only. When involving graph knowledge, the performance on the general domain task does not show apparent improvement, however on the specific domain task, a significant performance improvement has been observed. These results confirm the importance of learning with heterogeneous information resources.

The rest of the paper is organized as follows: Section 2 briefly describes the related works, Section 3 presents the joint learning approach. The experiments are presented in Section 4, and some discussions are in Section 5. Section 6 concludes the paper.

2 Related work

Many researches have been conducted to learn semantic relevance from raw text data, labeled text data or graph knowledge bases. Most of the studies learn from single information resource.

For raw text learning, various unsupervised learning algorithms have been proposed to learn word representations from large-scale raw text (Huang et al., 2012; Mikolov et al., 2013; Pennington et al., 2014). These methods hypothesize that statistics of word co-occurrences in contexts involve rich semantic and syntactic information and can be utilized to embed words and/or phrases.

Some approaches have been presented to learn with raw text and labeled text together. Gabrilovich and Markovitch (2007) introduced the explicit semantic analysis which represents a word by its distribution over the labeled wikipedia pages instead of the latent concepts as in LSA (Deerwester et al., 1990) and LDA (Blei et al., 2003). Its great performance owes to learning from the combination of raw text and labeled text (wiki pages labeled by entries) resources. Recently, paragraph vector (PV) was also applied to semantic relevance tasks (Dai et al., 2014), which infers word vectors and paragraph vectors together, as the joint text learning presented in this study.

In the field of relevance learning with graph knowledge, early studies focused on measuring word similarity based on the graph theory, for instance, (Rada et al., 1989; Wu and Palmer, 1994; Resnik, 1995). Recent studies focus on various distributed representation models which embed entities and relations of large knowledge graph databases into a low-dimensional continuous space (Bordes et al., 2013; Socher et al., 2013; Fan et al., 2015).

Various approaches have been proposed to utilize heterogeneous resources. Recently, Riedel et al. (2013) demonstrated that text data can help discovering new relation in graph completing task. Weston et al. (2013) used text data for the same purpose while they used word vectors that may leverage text resources more effectively.

Most recently, joint learning approaches have been proposed to learn from heterogeneous resources. Yu and Dredze (2014) learned word vectors by considering not only the word context in text data but also relations in knowledge bases. Their training algorithm draws close the words that are proximate in both text and the knowledge graph. Xu et al. (2014) considered relation types in the joint training process. Faruqui et al. (2014) learned lexicon knowledge by forcing each word in the lexicon to be close to the corresponding pretrained word vector. These studies demonstrated that learning word vectors with both text data and graph knowledge is beneficial to semantic relevance learning.

This study is an extension to the existing joint learning methods. Particularly, we also learn knowledge embedding from descriptions(labeled text). This is contrary to most of the existing researches which learn the knowledge only from context and knowledge graph. Additionally, a new joint learning framework is presented in this work, which integrates text and graph learning as a unified learning processing. Moreover, the contributions of different resources in different situations will be investigated.

3 Method

This section first presents the joint text learning approach which learns entity vectors based on the descriptions that are extracted from Wikipedia. Then the graph knowledge learning is described. Finally the joint text and graph learning is presented which learns with both text data and graph knowledge.

3.1 Joint text learning

Learning entity vectors with raw text can be simply implemented by treating entities as words (or phrases) and learning them together with other words. There are a number of approaches to learning word vectors (Huang et al., 2012; Mikolov et al., 2013; Pennington et al., 2014). In this study, the skip-gram model implemented in the word2vec tool[1] is adopted.

The simple approach to learning with labeled text is to average the vectors of words involved in the description of the current entity e. This is formulated by:

$$v_e = \frac{1}{|D_e|} \sum_{w \in D_e} v_w$$

where v_e denotes the vector of entity e, and v_w denotes the vector of word w. D_e represents set of word tokens within the description of e, and $|D_e|$ represents the size of D_e.

A better approach is to learn word and entity vectors simultaneously. The training is based on negative sampling (Mikolov et al., 2013), with the cost function defined as follows:

$$\mathcal{L}^{txt} = \sum_{e \in E} \sum_{i=1}^{K} max\{0,\ \gamma_{txt} - v_e^T v_{w_i} + v_e^T v_{w_i'}\}$$

where E is the set of entities to learn, and γ_{txt} is the boundary margin which has been empirically set to 0.5 in this study. (w_i, w_i') is a pair of words for which w_i is sampled from the description of entity e, and w_i' is sampled from a proposal distribution. w_i is constrained to be different each time of sampling for a particular entity. K is the number of samples for each entity. In our study, K is set to 30 unless the description is shorter than 30 words. The proposal distribution for sampling w_i' is set to be the unigram distribution of all the words involved in the descriptions of all the entities. We call this model the joint text learning model. The stochastic gradient descendent (SGD) algorithm is employed to optimize $\mathcal{L}^{txt}$ with respect to the entity and word vectors.

Note that this model is similar to PV-DBOW, a distributed bag-of-words model proposed by Le and Mikolov (2014). In PV-DBOW, paragraphs are represented by paragraph vectors (PV) and are trained together with word vectors. The PVs correspond to the entity vectors in our model. A main difference between our model and the PV-DBOW model is that the cost function of our model is based on the hinge loss, while PV-DBOW uses the softmax function. This new cost function provides almost the same performance but offers a lower computation complexity because we don't need to count the sum of distances of the whole dictionary (which is what softmax does).

[1] http://code.google.com/p/word2vec

In the experiments, word vectors that are pre-trained with raw text are used to initialize the entity vectors. This pre-training leads to a big improvement compared with random initialization, as will be shown in Section 4.

3.2 Graph knowledge learning

As mentioned in Section 1, knowledge bases such as WordNet and Yago contain plenty of entities and their relations, leading to complex knowledge graphs. Since these entities and relations are annotated by people, graph knowledge is highly reliable and can be used to embed entities. Note that different knowledge bases contain different types of relations. For WordNet, nearly half of the relations are the hypernym-hyponym (is-a) relation, and for Freebase, the relation types are much more complicated. Although it is possible to learn different relations (Bordes et al., 2013), this study does not consider it since our focus is semantic relatedness instead of relation prediction. More discussions about relation type learning will be given in Section 5.

For this reason, only entity vectors are learned (the global relation vector can be absorbed into the entity vectors). This is similar to the unstructured model in Bordes's early work (Bordes et al., 2013), except that distance between vectors is measured by inner product in our model, while Bordes's work used Euclidean distance. We make this choice for two reasons: firstly, to make the graph knowledge learning consistent with the joint text learning so that their results are comparable, and more importantly they can be combined into a joint text and graph learning as will be presented in the next section; secondly, word vectors trained with raw text can be used to pre-train (initialize) the entity vectors, which has been demonstrated to be highly effective, as will be seen in Section 4.

Similar to the text learning, the negative sampling approach is used to train the model. Denote the related entity pairs defined by the knowledge base by $P = \{P_i; P_i = (e_i^l, e_i^r)\}$. For each pair P_i, the negative sampling corrupts the pair by replacing either the left entity e_i^l or the right entity e_i^r with a randomly selected entity. The learning optimizes the following hinge loss function:

$$\mathcal{L}^{grh} = \sum_{P_i \in P} max\{0, \gamma_{grh} - {v_{e_i^l}}^T v_{e_i^r} + {v_{e'^l_i}}^T v_{e'^r_i}\}$$

where γ_{grh} is the boundary margin which is empirically set to 1.0 in this study, and $({e'}_i^l, {e'}_i^r)$ is the corrupted version of (e_i^l, e_i^r) (only one entity corrupted). Again, the SGD algorithm is used to optimize $\mathcal{L}^{grh}$ with respect to the entity vectors.

3.3 Joint text and graph learning

The joint text learning and the graph knowledge learning can be combined. In fact, the two learning approaches are based on the same measure space (the inner product space) and the objective functions are both hinge loss; additionally, both the learning methods train the model using SGD and negative sampling. This means that they are highly consistent and can be easily combined without much change, except that the objective function is modified to integrate the loss derived from both text and graph knowledge. This is formulated by:

$$\mathcal{L}^{joint} = \mathcal{L}^{txt} + \beta \mathcal{L}^{grh} \quad (1)$$

where β is a hyper-parameter that is set to balance the contributions of the text data and the graph knowledge. The SGD algorithm is employed to optimize $\mathcal{L}^{joint}$ with respect to the entity vectors and the vectors of words that are involved in the entity descriptions. In practice, an iterative strategy is adopted in this work, which performs the joint text learning and the graph knowledge training alternatively and iteratively, with their respective negative sampling schemes applied.

4 Experiments

This section reports the experimental settings and results. The semantic relatedness task was chosen in the study, which measures semantic relatedness among entities and compare the measurements with human-specified scores. We start by presenting the databases, and then report the results on a general domain task and a specific domain task. The data sets and codes are available online. [2]

4.1 Databases

Training data

Three information resources are used in the experiments: Wikipedia as the raw and labeled text, Wordnet and Yago as the graph knowledge. Wikipedia[3] is a free-access, free content internet encyclopedia which at present contains more than 4.7 millions of English entries. Wikipedia itself offers plenty of information, including the main

[2] `http://git.cslt.org/zhangdx/jointsemanticlearning`

[3] `http://wikipedia.org`

content in plain text (description), category information, links to other entries, and info-boxes. Only the plain text and the entry name (title) of descriptions are used in this study. WordNet (Fellbaum, 1998) is a well-known semantic knowledge base which contains 117k English words and the associated information such as brief text descriptions and relations. Yago (Fabian et al., 2007) is another popular semantic knowledge base, derived from Wikipedia, WordNet and GeoNames.

The training (entity vector embedding) is conducted on two development data sets: a subset of entities of WordNet that involves only nouns (WNet-N) and a subset of entities of Yago that involves animal names (Yago-A). WNet-N can be regarded as a data set in the general domain, while Yago-A is a data set in a particular domain. For each entity in the two data sets, the corresponding wiki page is retrieved from Wikipedia, from which the plain text is retrieved and used as the labeled text for the entity. The plain text of all the entities in WNet-N and Yago-A are used as raw text. More details of the data sets are described as follows.

- WNet-N: A subset of WordNet which contains 68569 entities and 70040 relation pairs. All the entities are nouns and are words or phrases in the general domain. 36519 entities find their text descriptions in Wikipedia (labeled text), resulting in 111MB raw text.

- Yago-A: A subtree of Yago which contains 39900 entities, 72936 relation pairs. All the entities are Animal names, which means the entities are domain-specific. 6415 entities find their text descriptions (labeled text), resulting in 19MB raw text.

Note that both WNet-N and Yago-A maintain a connected graph structure which means that for any two entities in the graph, there is at least one path that connects them. This enables the simple connection-based relevance inference which derives relateness of two entities as the connection strength between them in the knowledge graph. Section 5 will compare this simple approach with our proposal.

Test data

As mentioned, this study chooses the semantic relatedness task to evaluate the performance of learned entity vectors. This task computes the relevance (distance) of two entities and then compares the resulting relevance score with the human-specified score. The Spearman coefficient is a widely-adopted metric to evaluate correlation between two variables and is used in this study to measure the consistence of the derived relevance with the human specification.

To test the performance on WNet-N, a subset of WordSimilarity-353[4] is used. The WordSimilarity-353 collection is a well-known test set for semantic relatedness tasks, which contains 353 word pairs and the relatedness scores of all the pairs are manually annotated. After filtering out the words that are absent from the entities of WNet-N, the resulted 301 pairs are used as the test set, named as Sim-301 in the following sections.

For the test on Yago-A, we propose a new test set Animal-143, which contains 143 pairs of common animal names and 92 different animals including mammals, birds, insects and marine animals. All the names are entities of Yago-A. The relatedness score of each pair has been evaluated by 9 persons, and the average is used as the human judgement. The range of score is from 0 to 3. For instance, the score between antelope and swan should probably be 0, and the score between cattle and bison can be 3. Table 1 summarizes the data sets used in the experiments.

4.2 Individual learning

The first experiment studies the performance of learning with raw text, labeled text and graph knowledge individually. As mentioned already, the test are conducted on two data sets: WNet-N and Yago-A, which represent a general domain task and a specific domain task, respectively. The impact of the dimension of the entity vectors is also investigated. The results in terms of Spearman coefficients are reported in Table 2.

For the raw text learning, the entities are treated as words or word sequences (phrases). The vectors of these words and word sequences are then learned by the word2vector tool, together with other words. The raw text data of WNet-N and Yago-A are merged, and combined with additional 200MB plain text to form a training data set to conduct the word vector training. Using the text of both the two data sets is to demonstrate the advantage that word vectors can be learned with out-of-domain data. Note that multi-word entities can be learned as phrase vectors (Mikolov et al., 2013), though this is not considered in this study since the two test sets Sim-301 and Animal-143 contain only single-word entities. The results with

[4] http://www.cs.technion.ac.il/~gabr/resources/data/wordsim353/

Training Set	Graph Knowledge	labeled Text	Raw Text	Test Set
WNet-N	68569 entities 70040 relations	36519 entities	111MB	Sim-301
Yago-A	39900 entities 72936 relations	6415 entites	19MB	Animal-143

Table 1: Data sets for knowledge embedding and relatedness test.

raw text learning are reported in the row denoted by 'Word2vec' in Table 2.

For the labeled text learning, the entity vectors are derived as the mean vectors of the words involved in the text descriptions. This approach in fact involves both raw text learning (for word vectors) and labeled text learning (vector average), however the main knowledge source is the entity labels of the descriptions. The results with labeled text learning are reported in the row denoted by 'LT-mean' in Table 2.

Different from the mean-vector approach which first trains word vectors and then derives entity vectors, the joint text learning learns word vectors and entity vectors together. Two configurations are tested: in JT-rand, the entity vectors are randomly initialized, while in JT-prt, the entity vectors are initialized (pre-trained) by corresponding word vectors. Note that all the multi-word entities can not be pre-trained as the phrase vectors are not trained, however this does not much impact the resulting performance since the test sets do not involve multi-word entities.

For the graph knowledge learning, two configurations have been tested as well: with and without pre-training. For those entities that can't be pre-trained, random initialization is employed. The results are reported in the rows denoted by 'GR-rand' and 'GR-prt' in Table 2, for the configurations with and without pre-training, respectively.

From the results, it can be observed that the three learning approaches behave differently on the two test sets. The text-based learning exhibits clear advantage compared to graph knowledge learning on the WNet-N test, however on the Yago-A test, the graph knowledge learning is superior. This can be explained by the fact that WNet-N is in the general and involves popular entities that can be well trained with raw and labeled text, however for Yago-A, most of the entities are domain-specific and so it is not easy to learn the entities (and their relations) from unstructured text data. In this case, the human-specified knowledge, i.e., the relations offered by the graph knowledge, tends to provide the most valuable information. On the other hand, the graph knowledge of the general domain tends to be sparse and noisy, which will be discussed in Sec 5, while the graph knowledge of specific domains are generally less sparse and also quite clean. This also leads to more reliable inference with graph knowledge in specific domains.

Another observation is that the dimension of the entity vectors indeed impacts the performance. A larger dimension tends to perform better, at the cost of higher complexity in model training. In the following experiments, the dimension will be set to 100.

It can be also observed that the mean vector (LT-mean) approach does not work well, probably due to the information loss with the simple average. The joint text learning with pre-training (JT-prt) outperforms both LT-mean and Word2Vec. As JT-prt makes use of both raw text and labeled text, this superiority confirms that learning with heterogeneous information resources is beneficial, and the joint learning (JT-prt) is an appropriate way to utilize heterogeneous information effectively.

Finally, it can be seen that the pre-training with word vectors (trained with raw text) contributes to both the text learning and the graph knowledge learning: the pre-trained systems (JT-prt and GR-prt) significantly outperform the random initialized systems (JT-rand and GR-rand). This from another perspective confirms the importance of involving multiple and heterogeneous information resources in knowledge embedding. In addition, the poor performance of JT-rand is mainly due to the incompleteness and bias of descriptions. And the bad results on GR-rand are probably caused by the loss of relation types in databases and also the loss of the variation of length on edges since every edge is trained equally. Thus, pre-training method helps a lot since additional knowledge can be added in and the incompleteness of both description and graph can be hugely solved.

4.3 Joint text and graph learning

This section reports the experiment with the joint text and graph learning. From the experimental re-

Model	Spearman Coefficient					
	WNet-N			Yago-A		
	50	100	200	50	100	200
Word2vec	0.700	0.720	0.729	0.668	0.681	0.704
LT-mean	0.084	0.091	0.083	0.366	0.421	0.470
JT-rand	0.421	0.447	0.422	0.436	0.466	0.449
JT-prt	**0.726**	**0.744**	**0.749**	0.677	0.704	0.719
GR-rand	0.119	0.178	0.180	0.305	0.303	0.410
GR-prt	0.644	0.690	0.690	**0.726**	**0.727**	**0.718**

Table 2: Experimental results with raw text learning, labeled text learning, joint text learning and graph knowledge learning. Bold numbers shows the highest performance in each column.

sults of the previous section, it has been found that learning with multiple resources is helpful, even if with the simple pre-training. The joint text and graph learning takes into account both word contexts and relations when learning the entity vectors, and so may utilize text data and graph knowledge in a more effective way.

Figure 1 presents the experimental results with the joint text and graph learning. The two curves present the Spearman coefficients on WNet-N and Yago-A respectively. The learning rate of the SGD algorithm is set to 0.01, and the iteration number is set to 200. The dimension of the entity vectors and word vectors is set to 100. According to the cost function (1), the learning is impacted by the hyper-parameter β, so the results with various values of β are reported in Figure 1.

From the results presented in Figure 1, very different patterns on the two test sets are observed: for WNet-N, the best β is close to 0.0, which means that involving graph knowledge in the learning simply reduce the performance. However for Yago-A, the best β is around 1.0, which means that to achieve the best performance, the contribution from text and graph resources should be balanced. This discrepancy on the optimal β can be explained in the same way as in the previous experiment, that Yago-A is a specific domain test so that the entities can not be well trained by either text data or graph knowledge, so the two resources need to be utilized together, which is where the joint training contributes. In practical applications, people should increase the β when domain becomes narrow.

4.4 Performance comparison

The joint text and graph learning with the individual learning methods are compared in Table 3, where the optimal values of β (0.0 for WNet-N and 1.0 for Yago-A) have been applied. It can be

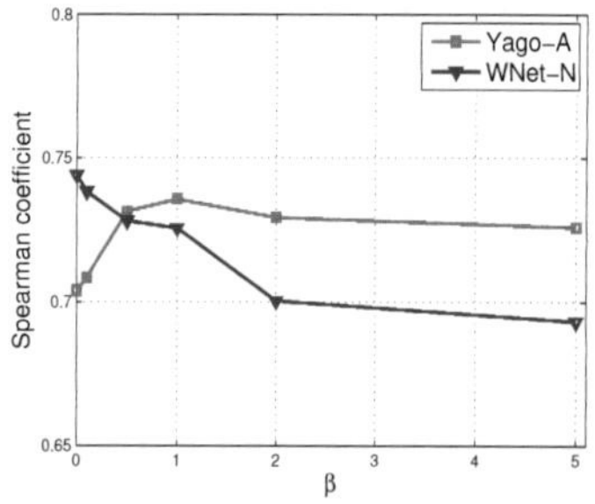

Figure 1: Experimental results with joint text and graph learning, with various values of β.

seen that the joint learning contributes significantly to the specific domain task on Yago-A, while for the general domain task on WNet-N, no improvement is found. Nevertheless, since the individual learning is a special case of the joint learning, the latter should be not worse than the former, given that the optimal β is applied.

Model	Spearman Coefficient	
	WNet-N	Yago-A
Word2vec	0.720	0.681
JT-prt	0.744	0.704
GR-prt	0.690	0.727
JTGR-prt	**0.744**	**0.735**

Table 3: Experimental results with joint text and graph learning, where β has been optimized.

5 Discussion

5.1 Performance of graph knowledge learning on different domains

In Section 4, it has been found that graph knowledge training does not work well on the general domain task WNet-N (refer to Table 2). This is possibly caused by the incompleteness of relations when domain becomes wider and the loss of the variation of length on edges in the knowledge base since every edge is trained equally. Notice that, the number of relation pairs in WNet-N is close to Yago-A while entities in WNet-N is more than entities in Yago-A. To further investigate the problem, two simple 'direct inference' algorithms are employed to conduct the tests on WNet-N and Yago-A respectively. The first algorithm is based on the shortest path between two entities in query, and the second one is Wu&Palmer's model (1994) which considers not only the shortest path but also the depth of their common parents. Note that both these two models do not learn any entity vectors but infer relatedness from the relations in the knowledge base, so the results can reflect the quality of the knowledge base.

The results are presented in Table 4. It can be seen clearly that both the shortest-path approach and Wu&Palmer's model show much better performance on Yago-A than on WNet-N. These results provide strong evidence that the general domain is much more complicated, so that the lack of graph knowledge and the problem caused by identical length of edges will easily hurt graph-based inference.

It is also clear that the two direct inference approaches outperform the graph learning approach when no pre-training applied, however with pre-training, the graph learning approach is much more superior, particularly for the WNet-N task. This suggests that learning with broad domain knowledge base is pretty hard, and extra information from raw text is essentially important.

Model	Spearman Coefficient	
	WNet-N	Yago-A
Shortest path	0.312	0.638
Wu&Palmer	0.338	0.662
GR-random	0.178	0.303
GR-prt	0.690	0.727

Table 4: Experimental results with various graph-based entity relateness inference methods.

5.2 Relation type learning

In our experiments, all the relations in the graph knowledge bases are treated indifferently. One may argue that different types of relations should be distinguished and learned distinctively. This is true for some tasks such as relation prediction; however, for the semantic learning task, it is still challenging to use relation information.

Table 5 presents the results with TransE as the graph knowledge learning using all the relation pairs from prolog of WordNet 3.0 which includes 15 types of relations. Note that TransE learns different types of relations as different relation vectors. It can be seen that substituting with TransE has very little effect on performance in both graph knowledge learning (TransE-prt) and joint text and graph learning (JTGR-TransE-prt).

Model	Spearman
JT-prt	0.729
Gr-prt	0.723
TransE-prt	0.726
JTGR-prt	0.739
JTGR-TransE-prt	0.740

Table 5: Performance with TransE in graph knowledge learning.

This can be explained as follows. Intuitively, when people evaluate the relatedness of two entities, both the relation types and the number of relations (directly and indirectly) between them are considered. Although different relation types may impact the judgement differently, learning relation types may force entity vectors to learn to distinguish different types of relations. This is an extra constraint that is irrelevant to our semantic relatedness task. If the constraint is too strong (TransE for example), it may lead to biased learning. Still, relations should be used, but maybe a weak constraint is more appropriate. This is one of the future work.

6 Conclusions

This paper presented a joint text and graph learning method which can learn entity vectors with text data and graph knowledge bases together. We evaluated the proposed method on the semantic relatedness task, and found that involving both text data and graph knowledge does improve performance. Particularly, the experimental results demonstrated that for general domain tasks, the graph knowledge tends to be incomplete thus learning with raw or labeled text is the most effective, however for specific domain tasks, the graph knowledge tends to be more complete, that it can contribute a lot to learning.

Acknowledge

This research was supported by the National Science Foundation of China (NSFC) under the project No. 61371136, and the MESTDC PhD Foundation Project No. 20130002120011. It was also supported by Sinovoice and Huilan Ltd.

References

David M Blei, Andrew Y Ng, and Michael I Jordan. 2003. Latent dirichlet allocation. *Journal of machine Learning research*, 3:993–1022.

Antoine Bordes, Nicolas Usunier, Alberto Garcia-Duran, Jason Weston, and Oksana Yakhnenko. 2013. Translating embeddings for modeling multi-relational data. In *Advances in Neural Information Processing Systems 26*, pages 2787–2795.

Andrew M Dai, Christopher Olah, Quoc V Le, and Greg S Corrado. 2014. Document embedding with paragraph vectors. In *NIPS 2014 in Deep Learning and Representation Learning Workshop*.

Scott C. Deerwester, Susan T Dumais, Thomas K. Landauer, George W. Furnas, and Richard A. Harshman. 1990. Indexing by latent semantic analysis. *Journal of The American Society for Information Science*, 41(6):391–407.

MS Fabian, K Gjergji, and W Gerhard. 2007. Yago: A core of semantic knowledge unifying wordnet and wikipedia. In *16th International World Wide Web Conference, WWW*, pages 697–706.

Miao Fan, Qiang Zhou, Andrew Abel, Thomas Fang Zheng, and Ralph Grishman. 2015. Probabilistic belief embedding for knowledge base completion. *CoRR*, abs/1505.02433.

Manaal Faruqui, Jesse Dodge, Sujay K Jauhar, Chris Dyer, Eduard Hovy, and Noah A Smith. 2014. Retrofitting word vectors to semantic lexicons. *arXiv preprint arXiv:1411.4166*.

Christiane Fellbaum. 1998. *WordNet*. Wiley Online Library.

Evgeniy Gabrilovich and Shaul Markovitch. 2007. Computing semantic relatedness using wikipedia-based explicit semantic analysis. In *Proceedings of the 20th International Joint Conference on Artificial Intelligence*, volume 7, pages 1606–1611.

Eric H Huang, Richard Socher, Christopher D Manning, and Andrew Y Ng. 2012. Improving word representations via global context and multiple word prototypes. In *Proceedings of the 50th Annual Meeting of the Association for Computational Linguistics: Long Papers-Volume 1*, pages 873–882. Association for Computational Linguistics.

Quoc V Le and Tomas Mikolov. 2014. Distributed representations of sentences and documents. In *Proceedings of The 31st International Conference on Machine Learning*, pages 1188–1196.

Tomas Mikolov, Ilya Sutskever, Kai Chen, Greg S Corrado, and Jeff Dean. 2013. Distributed representations of words and phrases and their compositionality. In *Advances in Neural Information Processing Systems 26*, pages 3111–3119.

Jeffrey Pennington, Richard Socher, and Christopher D Manning. 2014. Glove: Global vectors for word representation. *Proceedings of the Empiricial Methods in Natural Language Processing (EMNLP 2014)*, 12.

Roy Rada, Hafedh Mili, Ellen Bicknell, and Maria Blettner. 1989. Development and application of a metric on semantic nets. *Systems, Man and Cybernetics, IEEE Transactions on*, 19(1):17–30.

Philip Resnik. 1995. Using information content to evaluate semantic similarity in a taxonomy. In *In Proceedings of the 14th International Joint Conference on Artificial Intelligence*, pages 448–453.

Sebastian Riedel, Limin Yao, Andrew McCallum, and Benjamin M Marlin. 2013. Relation extraction with matrix factorization and universal schemas. In *Proceedings of NAACL-HLT*, pages 74–84.

Richard Socher, Danqi Chen, Christopher D Manning, and Andrew Ng. 2013. Reasoning with neural tensor networks for knowledge base completion. In *Advances in Neural Information Processing Systems 26*, pages 926–934.

Jason Weston, Antoine Bordes, Oksana Yakhnenko, and Nicolas Usunier. 2013. Connecting language and knowledge bases with embedding models for relation extraction. In *Proceedings of the Empiricial Methods in Natural Language Processing (EMNLP 2013)*, pages 1366–1371.

Zhibiao Wu and Martha Palmer. 1994. Verbs semantics and lexical selection. In *Proceedings of the 32nd annual meeting on Association for Computational Linguistics*, pages 133–138. Association for Computational Linguistics.

Chang Xu, Yalong Bai, Jiang Bian, Bin Gao, Gang Wang, Xiaoguang Liu, and Tie-Yan Liu. 2014. Rc-net: A general framework for incorporating knowledge into word representations. In *Proceedings of the 23rd ACM International Conference on Conference on Information and Knowledge Management*, pages 1219–1228. ACM.

Mo Yu and Mark Dredze. 2014. Improving lexical embeddings with semantic knowledge. In *Proceedings of the 52nd Annual Meeting of the Association for Computational Linguistics*, volume 2, pages 545–550.

Exploring the effect of semantic similarity for Phrase-based Machine Translation

Kunal Sachdeva, Dipti Misra Sharma
Language Technologies Research Centre, IIIT Hyderabad
kunal.sachdeva@research.iiit.ac.in, dipti@iiit.ac.in

Abstract

The paper investigates the use of semantic similarity scores as feature in the phrase based machine translation system. We propose the use of partial least square regression to learn the bilingual word embedding using compositional distributional semantics. The model outperforms the baseline system which is shown by an increase in BLEU score. We also show the effect of varying the vector dimension and context window for two different approaches of learning word vectors.

1 Introduction

The current state of the art Statistical Machine Translation (SMT) systems (Koehn et al., 2003) do not account for semantic information or semantic relatedness between the corresponding phrases while decoding the n-best list. The phrase pair alignments extracted from the parallel corpora offers further limitation of capturing contextual and linguistic information. Since the efficiency of statistical system depends on the quality of parallel corpora, low resourced language pair fails to meet the desired standards of translation.

Word representation is being widely used in many Natural Language Processing (NLP) applications like information retrieval, machine translation and paraphrasing. The word representation computed from continuous monolingual text provide useful information about the relationship between different words. Distributional semantics offers a notion of capturing semantic similarity between words occurring in similar context, where similar meaning words are grouped closely in a high dimension word space model. Each word is associated with an n-dimensional vector which represents its position in a vector space model and similar words are at small distance in comparison to relatively opposite meaning words.

The recent work in word vectors have shown to capture the linguistic relations and regularities. The relation between words can be expressed as a simple mathematical relation between their corresponding word vectors. The recent paper by Mikolov (Mikolov et al., 2013c) have shown through a word analogy task that the vec ("man") - vec ("woman") + vec("king") should be close to vec("queen"). Capturing of these relations along with word composition have shown significant improvements in various NLP and information retrieval tasks.

In this paper, we present our ideas of capturing the semantic similarity between phrase pairs in context of SMT and use the scores as features while decoding n-best list. We make use of word representations computed from two different methods: word2Vec (Mikolov et al., 2013a) and GloVe (Pennington et al., 2014) and show the effect of varying the context window and vector dimension for Hindi-English language pair. We use partial least squares (PLS) regression to learn the bilingual word embeddings using a bilingual dictionary, which is most readily available resource for any language pair. In this work we are not optimizing over the vector dimension and context window, but provide insights (through experiments) on how these two parameters effect the similarity tasks.

The rest of the paper is organized as follows. We first present the related work in vector space models and their utilization in machine translation domain (section 2). Section 3 describes the two methods we have adopted for computing word embeddings. The basic SMT setup, formulating transformation model and phrase similarity scores are described in section 4. In section 5 we present our results and conclude the paper in section 6 with some future directions.

Proceedings of the 3rd Workshop on Continuous Vector Space Models and their Compositionality (CVSC), pages 41–47,
Beijing, China, July 26-31, 2015.

2 Related Work

The current research community has shown special interest towards vector space models by organizing various dedicated workshops in top rated conferences. Word representations have been used in many NLP applications like information extraction (Paşca et al., 2006; Manning et al., 2008), sentiment prediction (Socher et al., 2011) and paraphrase detection (Huang, 2011).

In the past various methodologies have been suggested to learn bilingual word embeddings for various natural language related tasks. (Mikolov et al., 2013b) and (Zou et al., 2013) have shown significant improvements by using bilingual word embeddings in context of machine translation experiments. The former applies linear transformation to bilingual dictionary while the latter uses word alignments knowledge. Zhang (2014) proposed an auto-encoder based approach to learn phrase embeddings from the word vectors and showed improvements by using semantic similarity score in MT experiments. The phrase vector is generated by recursively combining the two children vector into a same dimensional parent vector using the method suggested by (Socher et al., 2011).

The work of (Gao et al., 2013) proposes a method for learning the semantic representation of phrase using features (multi-layer neural network) which is then used to compute the distance between them in a low dimensional space. The learning of weights in the neural network is guided by the BLEU score (ultimate goal to improve the quality of translation through increase in BLEU score) which makes it sensitive towards the score. Wu (2014) proposed an approach of using supervised model of learning context-sensitive bilingual embedding where the aligned phrase pairs are marked as true labels.

Since these defined methods depends heavily on the quality of word vectors, a number of approaches have been suggested in past to learn word representations from monolingual corpus: word2Vec (Mikolov et al., 2013a), GloVe (Pennington et al., 2014) and (Huang et al., 2012).

In this work, we extend the phrase similarity work by using the regression approach to learn the bilingual word embeddings. We employ vector composition approach to compute the phrase vector, where we add vectors of each constituent word to achieve the phrase vector. We also present the comparison of using different word embedding models along with varying context window and vector dimension which has not been shown (in detail) in any of the previous works. As pointed by (Mikolov et al., 2013b) linear transformation works well for language pairs which are closely related, however in this work we experiment with PLS regression which also establishes a linear relationship between words but is much more efficient than the simple least squares regression (explained in 4.2).

3 Learning word representation

We have used a part of WMT'14[1] monolingual data and news crawled monolingual data to learn word representations for English and Hindi respectively. We added the ILCI bilingual corpus (Jha, 2010) of English and Hindi to the monolingual data. The corpus statistics (after cleaning) are provided in table 1. The vocabulary refers to the words in embeddings with a minimum frequency of five within the corpus.

Language	# of Words	Vocabulary
English	250M	274K
Hindi	80M	184K

Table 1: Monolingual corpus statistics

3.1 word2Vec

The word2Vec model proposed by (Mikolov et al., 2013a) computes vectors by skip-gram and continuous bag of words (CBOW) model. These models use a single layer neural networks and are computationally much more efficient than any previously proposed model. The CBOW architecture of model predicts the current word based on the context whereas the skip-gram model predicts the neighboring words depending on the current word. Experiments have shown CBOW architecture to perform better on the syntactic task and skip-gram based architecture on the semantic tasks.

We have used the skip-gram architecture of word2Vec in our experiments as it has been shown to perform better for semantic related tasks.

3.2 GloVe

The Global Vector model of learning word representation was proposed by (Pennington et al., 2014) which computes the word vectors from a

[1] http://www.statmt.org/wmt14/translation-task.html

global word-word co-occurrence matrix. The relationship between words is extracted by using the ratio of co-occurrence probability with various probe words, which distinguishes between the relevant and irrelevant words. The co-occurrence probability of word *'i'* to that of word *'j'* is studied on the basis of a probe word *'k'* which is computed on the basis of a ratio P_{ik}/P_{jk}. The ratio is expected to be higher if word *'k'* is more related to word *'i* and low if it is related to word *'j'*. The author shows significant improvement over the word2Vec model on various NLP tasks (word similarity, word analogy and named entities recognition).

For training both the models we have altered the vector size and the context window, while all other parameters are set to default.

4 Experiments

4.1 Baseline MT System

We have used the ILCI corpora (Jha, 2010) which contains 50000 Hindi-English parallel sentences (49300 after cleaning) from health and tourism domains. The corpus is randomly split (equal variation of sentence length) into training (48300 sentences), development (500 sentences) and testing (500 sentences).

Division	# of sentences
Training	48300
Development	500
Testing	500

Table 2: MT system corpus statistics

We trained two Phrase based (Koehn et al., 2003) MT systems (Hindi - English and English - Hindi) using the Moses toolkit (Koehn et al., 2007) with phrase-alignments (maximum phrase length restricted to 4) extracted from GIZA++ (Och and Ney, 2000). We have used the SRILM (Stolcke and others, 2002) with Kneser-Ney smoothing (Kneser and Ney, 1995) for training a language model of order five and MERT (Och, 2003) for tuning the model with development data. We achieve a BLEU (Papineni et al., 2002) score of 19.89 and 22.82 on English-Hindi and Hindi-English translation systems respectively. These translation scores serves as our baseline for further experiments.

4.2 Partial Least Square (PLS) Regression

We generate the word embeddings of both Hindi and English using monolingual corpus using two previously mentioned methods (section 3). Since both the word embeddings are in different space (computed independently), there is a need to map the source vector space to target vector space or vice versa.

We employ the PLS (Abdi, 2003) regression to learn the transformation matrices. The observable variables (X) are the word embeddings of one language, while the predictable variables (Y) are the word embeddings of the other language. The observable and the predictable are $n \times d$ matrices, where 'n' is the number of words used (explained in subsection 4.3) and 'd' is the word embedding dimension. Our task is to compute a transformation matrix of $d \times d$ dimension which will be used to transform any given language word vector to its corresponding other language vector.

The PLS[2] regression algorithm works by projecting both X and Y matrices to a new space, and decomposes them into a set of orthogonal factors. The observables are first decomposed as $T = XW$ where 'T' and 'W' are the factor score matrix and weight matrix respectively. The predictable 'Y' is then estimated as $Y = TQ+E$ where 'Q' and 'E' are regression coefficient matrix and error term. We have the final regression model as $Y = XB+E$ where $B = WQ$ acts as our transformation matrix.

Dimension	word2Vec		GloVe	
	CW 5	CW 7	CW 5	CW 7
50	0.53	0.51	0.48	0.49
100	0.47	0.49	0.43	0.44
150	0.44	0.47	0.41	0.42
200	0.42	0.45	0.38	0.41
250	0.41	0.43	0.38	0.39
300	0.40	0.41	0.37	0.39
400	0.40	0.38	0.35	0.36
500	0.38	0.37	0.34	0.36

Table 3: Average word cosine similarity scores on test set. Context Window (CW)

4.3 Learning Transformation matrix

We employ PLS regression to learn bilingual word embeddings using a English-Hindi bilingual dictionary [3]. We have used 15000 words for train-

[2]http://www.statsoft.com/Textbook/Partial-Least-Squares
[3]http://www.shabdkosh.com/

ing the regression model and another set of 1500 words for testing purpose. The bilingual pair of training words are selected based on the frequency of those words occurring in a large plain text which consist of 10000 words from high frequency and 2500 words each of low and medium frequencies.

The observable variable and the predictable variables in the PLS regression are the word vectors of each word pair from their respective language word embedding models. We finally achieve two transformation models which transforms source to target vector space and target to source vector space. We have presented average similarity score on the test set in table 3 after transforming English words to Hindi word space.

4.4 Decoding with semantic similarity score

In the phrase based MT system we add two features (semantic similarity scores) to the bilingual phrase pairs. Since we need the vector representation of a phrase, we employ the works of (Mitchell and Lapata, 2008) on compositional semantics (adding the vectors) to compute the phrase representation. For a give phrase pair (s,t), we transform each constituent word of the source phrase *'s'* to the target word space and add the the transformed word embedding to the resultant source vector. We ignore the word if it does not occur in the word embeddings vocabulary. Similarly, we compute the phrase representation of the target phrase *'t'* by simply adding the word vectors to the resultant target vector. We then compute the cosine similarity between the two vectors which acts as a feature for the MT decoder. We also include the similarity score of transforming the target word phrase to source phrase as another feature. The phrase table is tuned with the previously used development data (development set used for tuning baseline MT system) using the MERT algorithm to compute the weight parameters for the baselines features and semantic similarity features.

5 Results and Discussion

The results of word similarity scores on the test set (bilingual dictionary words section 4.3) are presented in table 3 using the computed transformation matrix for English to Hindi. The similarity scores are continuously decreasing with increase in dimension, which shows that the proposed approach works better at lower dimensions for word similarity task. The word2Vec model is performing better than the GloVe model on word-similarity task. Within the same model the word2vec model with context window of five performs better than the model with context window of seven, while it is opposite for the GloVe model.

Dimension	Eng-Hin	Hin-Eng
50	19.69	**22.97**
100	19.39	22.69
150	19.58	**22.90**
200	19.80	**23.31**
250	**20.05**	**23.15**
300	**20.18**	**23.21**
400	19.75	**23.34**
500	19.37	**23.36**

Table 4: BLEU score of system using Word2Vec model with a context window of 5.

The results of our experiments (on the same test data used for evaluating the baseline MT systems) with varying dimensionality and context window are presented in table 4, 5, 6 and 7. Each of the bold marked values in the tables indicate an increase in BLEU score over the baseline. The figure 1, 2, 3 and 4 presents the comparison of BLEU score for each of the model. The highest BLEU score achieved for English-Hindi translation system is **20.53** (increase of **0.64** BLEU score over the baseline) using GloVe model with a 500 dimension vector and a context window of 5, whereas the highest score for Hindi-English system is **23.56** (increase of **0.74** BLEU score over the baseline) using word2Vec model and context window of 7. It is quite interesting to note that the increasing dimensionality and context window does not ensure increasing BLEU scores. It is evident that at a certain dimensionality the decoder algorithm (combining feature scores using log-linear model) can start distinguishing between the good and bad translations. The Hindi-English system shows improvements for almost all the cases, whereas English-Hindi system does not show similar behavior. Though the word similarity scores indicates better performance at lower dimensions, the MT experiments BLEU scores does follow the same trend. Since this language pair has not been widely explored, the results on word similarity and MT scores are not directly comparable to the earlier proposed methods.

Dimension	Eng-Hin	Hin-Eng
50	19.81	**22.93**
100	19.85	**23.01**
150	19.55	**23.29**
200	**20.37**	**22.85**
250	**20.36**	**23.16**
300	**20.02**	22.32
400	19.47	**23.13**
500	19.67	**23.56**

Table 5: BLEU score of system using Word2Vec model with a context window of 7.

Dimension	Eng-Hin	Hin-Eng
50	19.75	**23.41**
100	19.60	22.84
150	**20.28**	**23.08**
200	19.77	**22.93**
250	**20.04**	**23.30**
300	**19.97**	**23.17**
400	19.85	**22.93**
500	**20.53**	22.72

Table 6: BLEU score of system using GloVe model with a context window of 5.

Dimension	Eng-Hin	Hin-Eng
50	**20.35**	22.78
100	19.81	**23.27**
150	**20.12**	22.81
200	19.12	**23.16**
250	19.85	22.60
300	**19.88**	**23.29**
400	**20.07**	22.83
500	**20.01**	**23.07**

Table 7: BLEU score of system using GloVe model with a context window of 7.

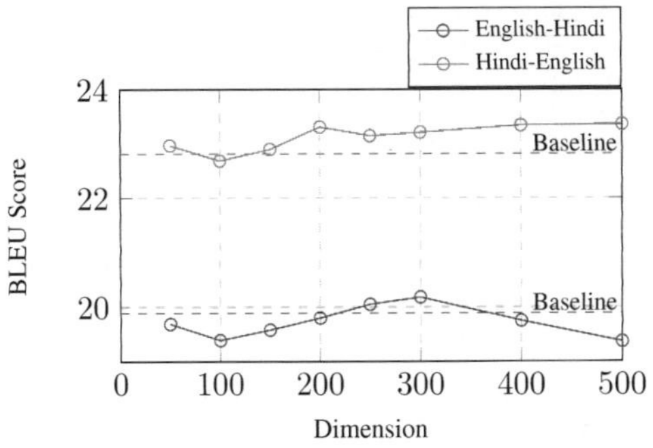

Figure 1: Plot of BLEU score variation using Word2Vec with a context window of 5

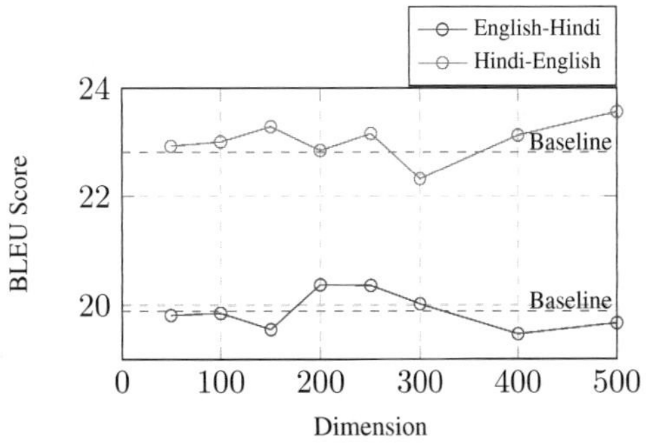

Figure 2: Plot of BLEU score variation using Word2Vec with a context window of 7

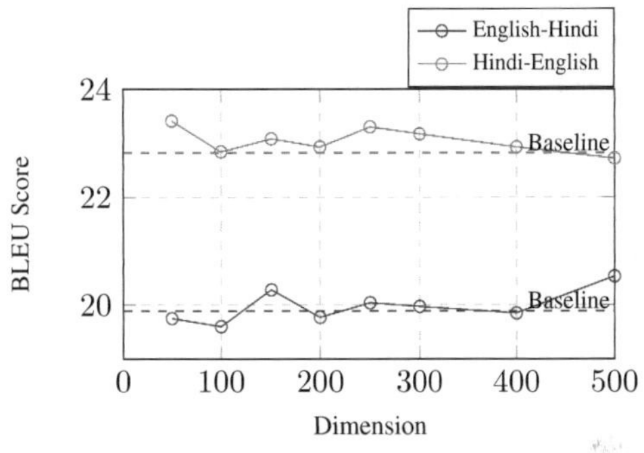

Figure 3: Plot of BLEU score variation using GloVe with a context window of 5

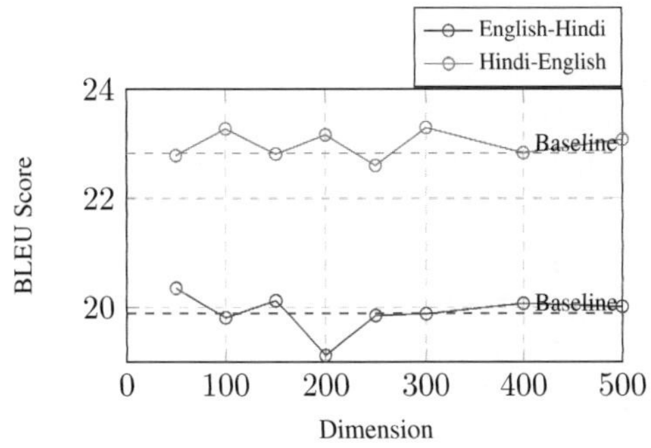

Figure 4: Plot of BLEU score variation using GloVe with a context window of 7

6 Conclusion and Future Work

In this paper we explore the use of semantic similarity between phrase pairs as features while decoding the n-best list. The bilingual word embeddings are learnt through PLS regression using a bilingual dictionary (which is an easily available resource considering low resourced language pairs as well) with limited vocabulary size. This method shows an increase in BLEU score for both English-Hindi and Hindi-English MT systems. This approach is quite effective in terms of overall complexity as the models developed by Zou (2013) and Zhang (2014) require much larger time for training.

As a part of future work, we propose the use of auto-encoders(Socher et al., 2011) to learn phrase representations as currently we are treating 'black'+'forest' and 'forest'+'black' to be having the same vector representation while semantically they are different . Since the words in one language can not be just linearly transformable to another language we will try to explore the use of feed-forward neural networks to learn non-linear transformations while minimizing the euclidean distance between the word embedding pairs. We also plan to extend the work by including the linguistic information in the word embeddings and taking the advantage of Hindi being a morphologically rich language.

References

Hervé Abdi. 2003. Partial least squares regression (pls-regression).

Jianfeng Gao, Xiaodong He, Wen-tau Yih, and Li Deng. 2013. Learning semantic representations for the phrase translation model. *arXiv preprint arXiv:1312.0482*.

Eric H Huang, Richard Socher, Christopher D Manning, and Andrew Y Ng. 2012. Improving word representations via global context and multiple word prototypes. In *Proceedings of the 50th Annual Meeting of the Association for Computational Linguistics: Long Papers-Volume 1*, pages 873–882. Association for Computational Linguistics.

Eric Huang. 2011. Paraphrase detection using recursive autoencoder.

Girish Nath Jha. 2010. The tdil program and the indian language corpora initiative (ilci). In *Proceedings of the Seventh Conference on International Language Resources and Evaluation (LREC 2010). European Language Resources Association (ELRA)*.

Reinhard Kneser and Hermann Ney. 1995. Improved backing-off for m-gram language modeling. In *Acoustics, Speech, and Signal Processing, 1995. ICASSP-95., 1995 International Conference on*, volume 1, pages 181–184. IEEE.

Philipp Koehn, Franz Josef Och, and Daniel Marcu. 2003. Statistical phrase-based translation. In *Proceedings of the 2003 Conference of the North American Chapter of the Association for Computational Linguistics on Human Language Technology-Volume 1*, pages 48–54. Association for Computational Linguistics.

Philipp Koehn, Hieu Hoang, Alexandra Birch, Chris Callison-Burch, Marcello Federico, Nicola Bertoldi, Brooke Cowan, Wade Shen, Christine Moran, Richard Zens, et al. 2007. Moses: Open source toolkit for statistical machine translation. In *Proceedings of the 45th Annual Meeting of the ACL on Interactive Poster and Demonstration Sessions*, pages 177–180. Association for Computational Linguistics.

Christopher D Manning, Prabhakar Raghavan, and Hinrich Schütze. 2008. *Introduction to information retrieval*, volume 1. Cambridge university press Cambridge.

Tomas Mikolov, Kai Chen, Greg Corrado, and Jeffrey Dean. 2013a. Efficient estimation of word representations in vector space. *arXiv preprint arXiv:1301.3781*.

Tomas Mikolov, Quoc V Le, and Ilya Sutskever. 2013b. Exploiting similarities among languages for machine translation. *arXiv preprint arXiv:1309.4168*.

Tomas Mikolov, Ilya Sutskever, Kai Chen, Greg S Corrado, and Jeff Dean. 2013c. Distributed representations of words and phrases and their compositionality. In *Advances in Neural Information Processing Systems*, pages 3111–3119.

Jeff Mitchell and Mirella Lapata. 2008. Vector-based models of semantic composition. In *ACL*, pages 236–244.

Franz Josef Och and Hermann Ney. 2000. Improved statistical alignment models. In *Proceedings of the 38th Annual Meeting on Association for Computational Linguistics*, pages 440–447. Association for Computational Linguistics.

Franz Josef Och. 2003. Minimum error rate training in statistical machine translation. In *Proceedings of the 41st Annual Meeting on Association for Computational Linguistics-Volume 1*, pages 160–167. Association for Computational Linguistics.

Kishore Papineni, Salim Roukos, Todd Ward, and Wei-Jing Zhu. 2002. Bleu: a method for automatic evaluation of machine translation. In *Proceedings of the 40th annual meeting on association for computational linguistics*, pages 311–318. Association for Computational Linguistics.

Marius Paşca, Dekang Lin, Jeffrey Bigham, Andrei Lifchits, and Alpa Jain. 2006. Names and similarities on the web: fact extraction in the fast lane. In *Proceedings of the 21st International Conference on Computational Linguistics and the 44th annual meeting of the Association for Computational Linguistics*, pages 809–816. Association for Computational Linguistics.

Jeffrey Pennington, Richard Socher, and Christopher Manning. 2014. Glove: Global vectors for word representation. *Proceedings of the Empiricial Methods in Natural Language Processing (EMNLP 2014)*.

Richard Socher, Jeffrey Pennington, Eric H Huang, Andrew Y Ng, and Christopher D Manning. 2011. Semi-supervised recursive autoencoders for predicting sentiment distributions. In *Proceedings of the Conference on Empirical Methods in Natural Language Processing*, pages 151–161. Association for Computational Linguistics.

Andreas Stolcke et al. 2002. Srilm-an extensible language modeling toolkit. In *INTERSPEECH*.

Haiyang Wu, Daxiang Dong, Wei He, Xiaoguang Hu, Dianhai Yu, Hua Wu, Haifeng Wang, and Ting Liu. 2014. Improve statistical machine translation with context-sensitive bilingual semantic embedding model. In *Proceedings of the 2014 Conference on Empirical Methods in Natural Language Processing (EMNLP)*, pages 142–146.

Jiajun Zhang, Shujie Liu, Mu Li, Ming Zhou, and Chengqing Zong. 2014. Bilingually-constrained phrase embeddings for machine translation. In *Proceedings of the 52th Annual Meeting on Association for Computational Linguistics. Association for Computational Linguistics*.

Will Y Zou, Richard Socher, Daniel M Cer, and Christopher D Manning. 2013. Bilingual word embeddings for phrase-based machine translation. In *EMNLP*, pages 1393–1398.

Incremental Adaptation Strategies for Neural Network Language Models

Aram Ter-Sarkisov, Holger Schwenk, Loïc Barrault and Fethi Bougares
School of Computer Science, University of Maine,
Le Mans, France
tersarkisovl@lium.univ-lemans.fr

Abstract

It is today acknowledged that neural network language models outperform back-off language models in applications like speech recognition or statistical machine translation. However, training these models on large amounts of data can take several days. We present efficient techniques to adapt a neural network language model to new data. Instead of training a completely new model or relying on mixture approaches, we propose two new methods: continued training on resampled data or insertion of adaptation layers. We present experimental results in an CAT environment where the post-edits of professional translators are used to improve an SMT system. Both methods are very fast and achieve significant improvements without over-fitting the small adaptation data.

1 Introduction

A language model (LM) plays an important role in many natural language processing applications, namely speech recognition and statistical machine translation (SMT). For a very long time, back-off n-gram models were considered to be the state-of-the-art, in particular when large amounts of training data are available.

An alternative approach is based on the use of high-dimensional embeddings of the words and the idea to perform the probability estimation in this space. By these means, meaningful interpolations can be expected. The projection and probability estimation can be jointly learned by a neural network (Bengio et al., 2003). These models, also called continuous space language models (CSLM), have seen a surge in popularity, and it was confirmed in many studies that they systematically outperform back-off n-gram models by a significant margin in SMT and speech recognition. Many variants of the basic approach were proposed during the last years, e.g. the use of recurrent architectures (Mikolov et al., 2010) or LSTM (Sundermeyer et al., 2012). More recently, neural networks were also used for the translation model in an SMT system (Le et al., 2012; Schwenk, 2012; Cho et al., 2014), and first translations systems entirely based on neural networks were proposed (Sutskever et al., 2014; Bahdanau et al., 2014).

However, to the best of our knowledge, all these systems are static, i.e. they are trained once on a large representative corpus and are not changed or adapted to new data or conditions. The ability to adapt to changing conditions is a very important property of an operational SMT system. The need for adaptation occurs for instance in a system to translate daily news articles in order to account for the changing environment. Another typical application is the integration of an SMT system in an CAT[1] tool: we want to improve the SMT systems with help of user corrections. Finally, one may also want to adapt a generic SMT to a particular genre or topic for which we lack large amounts of specific data. Various adaptation schemes were proposed for *classical SMT systems*, but to the best of our knowledge, there is only very limited works involving neural network models.

We are interested in a setting where an LM needs to be adapted to a small amount of data which is representative of a domain change, so that the overall system will perform better on this domain in the future. Our task, which corresponds to concrete needs in real-world applications, is the translation of a document by an human over several days. The human translator is assisted by an SMT system which proposes translation hypothesis to speed up his work (post editing). After one day of work, we adapt the CSLM to the transla-

[1] Computer Assisted Translation

Proceedings of the 3rd Workshop on Continuous Vector Space Models and their Compositionality (CVSC), pages 48–56,
Beijing, China, July 26-31, 2015.

tions already performed by the human translator, and show that the SMT system performs better on the remaining part of the document.

In this paper, we use the open-source MateCat tool[2] and a closely integrated SMT system[3] which is already adapted to the task (translation of legal documents). For each source sentence, the system proposes an eventual match in the translation memory and a translation by the SMT system. The human translator can decide to either post-edit them, or to perform a new translation from scratch. After one day of work, we want to use all the post-edited sentences to adapt the SMT systems, so that the translation quality is improved for the next day. This means that the SMT system will be adapted to the specific translation project. One important particularity of the task is that we have a very small amount of adaptation data, usually around three thousand words per day.

This paper is organized as follows. In the next two sections, we summarize basic notions of statistical machine translation and continuous space language models. We then present our tasks and results. The paper concludes with a discussion and directions of future research.

2 Related work

Popular approaches to adapt the LM in an SMT system are mixture models, *e.g.* (Foster and Kuhn, 2007; Koehn and Schroeder, 2007) and data selection. In the former case, separate LMs are trained on the available corpora and are then merged into one, the interpolation coefficients being estimated to minimize perplexity on an in-domain development corpus. This is known as linear mixture models. We can also integrate the various corpus-specific LMs as separate feature functions in the usual log-linear model of an SMT system.

Data selection aims at extracting the most relevant subset of all the available LM training data. The approach proposed in (Moore and Lewis, 2010) has turned out to be the most effective one in many settings. Adaptation of the LM of an SMT models in an CAT environment was also investigated in several studies, e.g. (Bach et al., 2009; Bertoldi et al., 2012; Cettolo et al., 2014).

Adaptation to new data was also investigated in the neural network community, usually by some type of incremental training on a (subset) of the data. Curriculum learning (Bengio et al., 2009), which aims in presenting the training data in a particular order to improve generalization, could be also used to perform adaptation on some new data. There are a couple of papers which investigate adaptation in the context of a particular application, namely image processing and speech recognition. One could for instance mention a recent work which investigated how to transfer features in convolutional networks (Yosinski et al., 2014), or research to perform speaker adaptation of a phoneme classifier based on TRAPS (Trmal et al., 2010).

There are also a few publications which investigate adaptation of neural network language models, most of them very recent. The insertion of an additional adaption layer to perform speaker adaptation was proposed by Park et al. (Park et al., 2010). Earlier this idea was explored in (Yao et al., 2012) for speech recognition through an affine transform of the output layer. Adaptation through data selection was studied in (Jalalvand, 2013) (selection of sentences in out-of-domain corpora based on similarity between sentences) and (Duh et al., 2013) (training of three models: n-gram, RNN and interpolated LM on two SMT systems: in-domain data only and all-domain). Several variants of curriculum learning are explored by Shi et al. to adapt a recurrent LM to a sub-domain, again in the area of speech recognition (Shia et al., 2014). Finally, one of the early applications of RNN was in (Kombrink et al., 2011): it was used to rescore the n-best list, speed-up the rescoring process, adapt an LM and estimate the influence of history.

3 Statistical Machine Translation

In the statistical approach to machine translation, all models are automatically estimated from examples. Let us assume that we want to translate a sentence in the source language s to a sentence in the target language $\mathbf{t}$. Then, the fundamental equation of SMT is, applying Bayes rule:

$$\mathbf{t}^* = \arg\max_{\mathbf{t}} P(\mathbf{t}|\mathbf{s}) = \arg\max_{\mathbf{t}} P(\mathbf{s}|\mathbf{t})P(\mathbf{t}) \quad (1)$$

The translation model $P(\mathbf{s}|\mathbf{t})$ is estimated from bitexts, bilingual sentence aligned data, and the language model $P(\mathbf{t})$ from monolingual data in the target language. A popular approach are phrase-based models which translate short sequences of words together (Koehn et al., 2003; Och and

[2]https://www.matecat.com/

[3]http://www.statmt.org/moses/

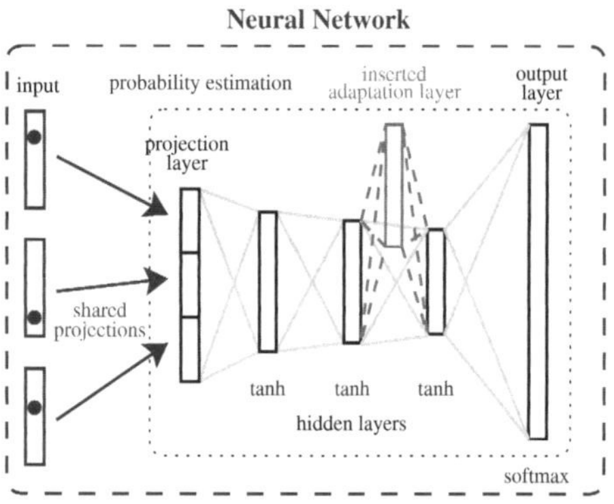

Figure 1: Basic architecture of an CSLM and insertion of an adaptation layer (dashed red).

Ney, 2003). The translation probabilities of these phrase pairs are usually estimated by simple relative frequency. The LM is normally a 4-gram back-off model. The log-linear approach is commonly used to consider more models (Och, 2003), instead of just a translation and language model:

$$\mathbf{t}^* = \arg\max_{\mathbf{t}} \sum_{m=1}^{M} \lambda_m h_m(\mathbf{s}, \mathbf{t}), \qquad (2)$$

where $h_m(\mathbf{s}, \mathbf{t})$ are so-called feature functions. The weights λ_m are optimized during the tuning stage. In the Moses system, fourteen feature functions are usually used.

Automatic evaluation of an SMT system remains an open question and many metrics have been proposed. In this study we use the BLEU score which measures the n-gram precision between the translation and a human reference translation (Papineni et al., 2002). Higher values mean better translation quality.

4 Continuous Space Language Model

The basic architecture of an CSLM is shown in Figure 1. The words are first projected onto a continuous representation, the remaining part of the network estimates the probabilities. Usually one tanh hidden and a softmax output layer are used, but recent studies have shown that deeper architecture perform better (Schwenk et al., 2014). We will use three tanh hidden and a softmax output layer as depicted in Figure 1. This type of architecture is now well known and the reader is referred to the literature for further details, e.g. (Schwenk, 2007).

All our experiments were performed with the open-source CSLM toolkit[4] (Schwenk, 2013), which was extended for our purposes. A major challenge for neural network LMs is how to handle the words at the output layer since a the softmax normalization would be very costly for large vocabularies. Various solutions have been proposed: short-lists (Schwenk, 2007), a class decomposition (Mikolov et al., 2011) or an hierarchical decomposition (Le et al., 2011). In this work, we use short-lists, but our adaptation scheme could be equally applied to the other solutions.

4.1 Adaptation schemes

As mentioned above, the most popular and most successful adaptation schemes for standard back-off LMs are data selection and mixture models. Both could be also applied to CSLMs. In practice, this would mean that we train a completely new CSLM on data selected by the adaptation process, or that we train several CSLMs, e.g. a generic and task-specific one, and combine them in linear or log-linear way. However, full training of an CSLM usually takes a substantial amount of time, often several hours or even days in function of the size of the available training data. Building several CSLMs and combining them would also increase the translation time.

Therefore, we propose and compare CSLM adaptation schemes which are very efficient: they can be performed in a couple of minutes. The underlying idea of both techniques is not to train new models, but to slightly change the existing CSLM in order to account for the new training data. In the first method, we perform **continued training** of the CSLM with a mixture of the new adaptation data and the original training data. In the second method, **adaptation layers are inserted** in the neural network as outlined in red in Figure 1. This additional layer is initialized with the identity matrix and only the weights of this layer are updated. This idea was previously proposed in framework of a speech recognition system (Park et al., 2010). We build on this work and explore different variants of this technique. An interesting alternative is to keep the original architecture of the NN and to only modify one layer, e.g. the weights between two tanh layers in Figure 1. This variant will be explored in future work.

[4]The CSLM toolkit is available at http://www-lium.univ-lemans.fr/~cslm/

Corpus	En/German	En/French
All data:		
Bitexts	129M	512M
Monolingual	643M	1300M
After data selection:		
Bitexts	49M	26M
Monolingual	44M	178M

Table 1: Statistics of the available resources (number of tokenized words)

5 Task and baselines

Our task is to improve an SMT system which is closely integrated into an open-source CAT tool with the post-edits provided by professional human translators. This tool and algorithms to update standard phrase-based SMT systems, including back-off language models, were developed in the framework of the European project MateCat (Cettolo et al., 2014). We consider the translation of legal texts from English into German and French. The available resources for each language pair are summarized in Table 1.

Each SMT system is based on the Moses toolkit (Koehn et al., 2007) and built according to the following procedure: first we perform data selection on the parallel and monolingual corpora in order to extract the data which is the most representative to our development set. In our case, we are interested in the translation of legal documents. Data selection is now a well established method in the SMT community. It is performed for the language and translation model using the methods described in (Moore and Lewis, 2010) and (Axelrod et al., 2011) respectively.

We train a 4-gram back-off LM and a phrase-based system using the standard Moses parameters. The coefficients of the 14 feature functions are optimized by MERT to maximize the BLEU score on the development data. This system is then used to create up to 1000 distinct hypotheses for each source sentence. We then add a 15th feature function corresponding to the log probability generated by CSLM for each hypothesis and the coefficients are again optimized. This is usually referred to as *n-best list rescoring*. We call this final system **domain-adapted** since it is optimized to translate legal documents. This system is then used to assist human translators to translate a large document in the legal domain.

Typically, we will process day by day: after one day of work, all the human translations (created from scratch or by post-editing the hypotheses from the SMT system) are injected into the system and we hope that SMT will perform better on the rest of the document to be translated, e.g. on the second day of work. This procedure can be repeated over several days when the document is rather large (see section 5.2). Usually humans are able to translate approximately 3 000 words per day. We call this procedure **project-adaptation**.

5.1 Results for the English/German system

The 4-gram back-off LM built on the selected data has a perplexity of 151.1 on the domain-specific development data. Given the fact that an CSLM can be very efficiently trained on long context windows, we used a 28-gram in all experiments. By these means we hope to capture the long range dependencies of German. The projection layer of the CSLM was of dimension 320, followed by three tanh hidden layers of size 1024 and a softmax output layer of 32k neurons (short-list). This short-list accounts for around 92 % of the tokens used in the corpus. The initial learning rate was set to 0.06 and exponentially decreased over the iterations. The network converged after 7 epochs with a perplexity of 96.6, *i.e.* a 36% relative reduction. The total training time is less than 7 hours on a Nvidia K20x GPU. Table 2 (upper part) gives the BLEU score of these baseline domain-adapted systems.

To analyze our project adaptation techniques we have split another legal document into two part, *"Day 1"* and *"Day 2"*. The first part, *"Day 1"*, containing around 3.2K words, is used to adapt the SMT system and the CSLM, aiming to improve the translation performance on the second part, named *"Day 2"*. Note that the performance on *"Day 1"* itself, after adaptation, is of limited interest since we could quite easily overtrain the model on this data. On the other hand, it is informative to monitor the performance on the domain-generic development set. Ideally, we will improve the performance on *"Day 2"*, *i.e.* future text of the same project than the adaptation data, with only a slightly loss on the generic development data.

Various adaptation schemes are compared in Table 4. The network is adapted on the data from *Day 1* and we want to improve performance on *Day 2*. At the same time, we do not want to

LM		BLEU score		
Approach	Adaptation	Dev	Day 1	Day 2
Domain adapted:				
Back-off	n/a	26.18	27.53	19.31
CSLM	n/a	26.89	27.14	20.28
Project adapted;				
Back-off	data selection	25.76	*(28.45)*	20.14
CSLM	none	26.45	*(28.65)*	20.57
	continued training	26.27	*(33.10)*	21.12
	additional layers	26.39	*(31.94)*	**21.26**

Table 2: Comparative BLEU scores for the English/German systems. Italic values in parenthesis are for information only. They are biased since the reference translations are used in training.

Percentage of adaptation data	Generic data (44M words)	Day 1 data (3.2k words)	# examples per epoch	training time per epoch
Domain-adapted CSLM:				
none	19.3M (42%)	n/a	19.3M	3250 sec
Project-adapted CSLM:				
14%	19 356 (0.042%)	3 220	22 576	3.5 sec
25%	9 696 (0.021%)	3 220	12 916	2.0 sec
45%	3 899 (0.008%)	3 220	7 119	1.1 sec
62%	1 967 (0.004%)	3 220	5 187	0.6 sec
77%	1 003 (0.002%)	3 220	4 223	0.5 sec

Table 3: English/German system: number of examples (28-grams) seen by the CSLM at each epoch. For the domain adapted system, we randomly resample about 42% of the examples at each epoch. For the project-adapted system, we experimented with various mixtures between generic and project specific data (Day 1). We don't want to train on Day 1 data only since this would result in strong over-fitting.

overfit the data and keep good performance on the domain-specific Dev set. To achieve this, we continued training of the networks with a mixture of old and new data. All the adaptation data was always used (*Day 1*, 3.2k words) and small fractions of the domain-selected data were randomly sampled at each epoch, so that the adaptation data accounts for 14, 25, 45, 62 and 77 % respectively. Since the networks are trained on very small amounts of data (4 - 23k words), the overall adaptation process takes only a few minutes. The statistics of the data used at each epoch is detailed in Table 3. We will show below that it is important to perform the adaptation of the CSLM with a mixture of generic and adaptation data to prevent overfitting.

We experiment along the following lines:

1. different resampling coefficients of adaptation and generic data according to Table 3.
2. network topologies:
   a) continue training of the original network updating all the weights.
   b) insert one or two hidden layers with 1024 neurons using linear or hyperbolic tangent activation functions respectively. These additional layers are initialized with the identity matrix and only these layers are updated using backpropagation function.

We record the perplexity of the adapted CSLM on *Day 2* ($\sim 11K$ words), which is then used as a guideline for selecting the best networks to integrate into an SMT system (marked with an asterisk in the Table 4). Lowest perplexity was obtained by keeping the baseline network topology (upper part of Table 4) when *Day 1* data constituted 14 % of the incremental training data set: the perplexity on *Day 2* decreases from 126.1 to 94.6, with a minor increase on the Dev set (96.6→98.7). Using larger

Network architecture	Updated layers	Activation function	Addtl. params	Percentage of adapt. data	Perplexity Day 2	Perplexity Dev
Original network architecture:						
1024-1024-1024 without adaptation	-	Tanh	-	-	126.1	96.6
1024-1024-1024 with incremental training	All	Tanh	-	14%	**94.6***	98.7
				25%	103.7	97.3
				45%	102.9	98.9
				62%	102.7	100.2
Insertion of an adaptation layer:						
1024-**1024**-1024-1024	inserted one only	Linear	1M	14%	106.0	97.4
				25%	104.9	99.5
1024-1024-**1024**-1024	inserted one only	Linear	1M	14%	103.8	98.8
				25%	97.9	102.5
1024-1024-1024-**1024**	inserted one only	Linear	1M	14%	101.2	100.8
				25%	102.2	104.1
1024-**1024**-1024-1024	inserted one only	Tanh	1M	14%	105.7	96.8
				25%	104.6	98.9
1024-1024-**1024**-1024	inserted one only	Tanh	1M	14%	103.5	96.4
				25%	102.6	98.4
1024-1024-1024-**1024**	inserted one only	Tanh	1M	14%	101.5	**95.1***
				25%	101.3	97.4

Table 4: Perplexities of CSLMs with one new hidden layer adapted to *Day 1*. Bold values in the architecture column are the new hidden layers. Bold values in the last two columns are the best perplexities for the respective test corpora. Tanh is a shorthand notation for the hyperbolic tangent activation function. Percentage is the proportion of *Day 1* data in the total corpora (see Table 3). All networks have been trained for 50 iterations.

fractions of *Day 1* leads to over-fitting of the network: the perplexity on *Day 2* and the generic Dev set increases.

The lower part of Table 4 summarizes the results when inserting one *adaptation layer*, with a linear or tanh activation function, at three different slots respectively. For each configuration, we explored five different proportions of the baseline corpora and *Day 1* (cf. Table 3), but for clarity, we only report the most interesting results. The overall tendency was that using more than 25% of *Day 1* systematically leads to over-fitting of the network. Several conclusions can be made: a) an tanh adaptation layer outperforms a linear one; b) it is better to insert the adaptation layer at the end of the network; c) updating the weights of the inserted layer only overfits less than incremental training the whole network (comparing the last block in Table 4 with the second block): the perplexity on *Day 1* decreases substantially (126.1→101.5) and we observe a slight improvement on the Dev set (96.6→95.1).

Finally, Table 2 lower part gives the BLEU scores of the project-adapted systems. When no CSLM is used, the BLEU score on Day 2 increases from 19.31 to 20.14 (+0.83). This is achieved by adapting the translation and back-off LM (details of the algorithms can be found in (Cettolo et al., 2014)). Both CSLM adaptation schemes obtained quite similar BLEU scores: 21.12 and 21.26 respectively, the insertion of one additional tanh layer having a slight advantage. Overall, the adapted CSLM yields an improvement of 1.12 BLEU (20.14 to 21.26) while it was about 1 point BLEU for the domain-adapted system (19.31 to 20.28). This nicely shows the effectiveness of our adaptation scheme, which can be applied in a couple of minutes.

5.2 Results for the English/French system

A second set of experiments was performed to confirm the effectiveness of our adaptation procedure on a different language pair: English/French. In the MT community it is well known that the translation into German is a very hard task which is reflected in the low BLEU scores around 20 (see Table 2). On the other hand, our baseline SMT system for the English/French language pair has a BLEU score well above 40. One may argue that it is more complicated to further improve such a system.

In addition, we investigate adaptation of the SMT system and the CSLM over five consecutive days: the human translator works for one day and corrects the SMT hypothesis, these corrections are used to adapt the system for the second day. Human corrections are again inserted into the system and a new system for the third day is built, and so on. With this adaptation scheme we want to verify whether our methods are robust or quickly overfit the adaptation data. The number of words for each day are about three thousand. A 16-gram CSLM for the French target language with a short-list of 12k was used. Training was performed for 15 epochs.

Day	Day 1	Days 1-2	Days 1-3	Days 1-4
1	39 %	27.9 %	21.6 %	17.7 %
2	-	29.6 %	22.9 %	18.8 %
3	-	-	22.3 %	18.1 %
4	-	-	-	17.4 %

Table 6: English/French task: proportion of each day in the adaptation data set, *e.g.* at the end of Day 2, we create an adaptation corpus which consists of 27.9% and 29.6% of data from Day 1 and Day 2 respectively, the remaining portions are randomly resampled in the training data.

For this task, we only used the incremental learning method (see Table 4) as it yielded the lowest perplexity in the English/German experiment. The data from the five consecutive days is coming from one large document which is assumed to be from one domain only. Therefore, we decided to always use all the available data from the preceding days to adapt our models. For instance, after the third day, the data from Day 1, 2 and 3 is used to build a new system for the fourth day. The proportions of each day in the corpus used to continue the training of the CSLM are given in Table 6 (note that every day's proportion decreases, but their combined share increases from 39% to 68%). The perplexities of the various CSLMs are given in Table 7.

Data	CSLM baseline	CSLM adapted
Day 1	233.9	-
Day 2	175.6	130.3
Day 3	153.0	130.2
Day 4	189.4	169.4
Day 5	189.2	167.7

Table 7: English/French task: perplexities of baseline and adapted CSLM (on all preceding days), *e.g.* the CSLM tested on Day 4 is the baseline CSLM that had been adapted with Days 1-3.

One first observation is the rather high perplexity of the models on each day. This shows the importance of project adaptation even when domain related data is available. Adaptation allows to decrease the perplexity by more than 10% relative for each day. While the perplexities vary between the project days, they are reduced in every case, which demonstrates the effectiveness of the adaptation method.

In order to evaluate the impact of the CSLM adaptation on the SMT system, we performed various translation experiments. The results are provided in Table 5. The BLEU scores of the various systems using the baseline and the adapted CSLMs are presented. We run tests with three different human translators - for the sake of clarity, we provide detailed results for one translator only. The observed tendencies are similar for the two other translators. First of all, one can see that the CSLM improves the BLEU score of the baseline systems between 2.3 to 3.4 BLEU points, *e.g.* for Day 2 from 44.07 to 46.61. Adapting the whole SMT system to the new data improves significantly the translation quality, *e.g.* from 46.61 to 52.01 for Day 2, without changing the CSLM. The proposed adaptation scheme of the CSLM achieves additional important improvements, in average 2.6 BLEU points. This gain is relatively constant for all days.

For comparison, we also give the BLEU scores when using four reference translations: the one of the three human translators and one independent translation which was provided by the European Commission.

We still observe some small gains although three out of four translations were not used in the adaptation process. This shows that our adaptation scheme not only learns the particular style of one

Approach	Day 1	Day 2	Day 3	Day 4	Day 5
Baseline SMT system:					
back-off LM	48.84/63.69	44.07/62.13	46.88/67.14	43.22/64.74	47.77/67.07
CSLM	52.25/67.04	46.61/65.64	49.73/70.70	45.68/68.61	50.06/69.70
Adapted SMT system:					
baseline CSLM	n/a	52.01/66.68	57.35/75.31	54.99/71.88	59.11/74.49
adapted CSLM		54.61/67.97	60.23/75.90	57.19/72.05	61.83/5.21
Improvement obtained by adapted CSLM		2.60/1.29	2.88/0.56	2.20/0.17	2.72/0.72

Table 5: BLEU scores obtained by a baseline SMT (without and with an CSLM) and a project-adapted SMT with baseline (unadapted) CSLM and adapted CSLM. The first value in every cell is the BLEU score obtained with respect to the reference translation of the human translator; the second one is calculated with respect to all the 3 references created by the professional translators (*i.e.* obtained by post-edition) and an independent reference.

translator, but also achieves more `generic` improvements. This also shows that the adaptation process is beneficial for improving state-of-the-art systems which already perform very well on certain tasks.

6 Conclusions

In this paper, we presented a thorough study of different techniques to adapt a continuous space language model to small amounts of new data. In our case, we want to integrate user corrections so that a statistical machine translation system performs better on similar texts. Our task, which corresponds to concrete needs in real world applications, is the translation of a document by an human over several days. The human translator is assisted by an SMT system which proposes translation hypothesis to speed up his work (post editing). After one day of work, we adapt the CSLM to the translations already performed by the human translator, and show that the SMT system performs better on the remaining part of the document.

We explored two adaptation strategies: continued training of an existing neural network LM, and insertion of an adaptation layer with the weight updates being limited to that layer only. In both cases, the network is trained on a combination of adaptation data (3–15k words) and a portion of similar size, randomly sampled in the original training data. By these means, we avoid overfitting of the neural network to the adaptation data. Overall, the adaptation data is very small – less than 50k words – which leads to very fast training of the neural network language model: a couple of minutes on a standard GPU.

We provided experimental evidence of the effectiveness of our approach on two large SMT tasks: the translation of legal documents from English into German and French respectively. In both cases, significantly improvement of the translation quality was observed.

References

Amittai Axelrod, Xiaodong He, and Jianfeng Gao. 2011. Domain adaptation via pseudo in-domain data selection. In *EMNLP*, pages 355–362.

Nguyen Bach, Roger Hsiao, Matthias Eck, Paisarn Charoenpornsawat, Stephan Vogel, Tanja Schultz, Ian Lane, Alex Waibel, and Alan W. Black. 2009. Incremental Adaptation of Speech-to-Speech Translation. In *NAACL*, pages 149—-152, Boulder, US-CO.

D. Bahdanau, K. Cho, and Y. Bengio. 2014. Neural machine translation by jointly learning to align and translate. In *NIPS workshop on Modern Machine Learning and Natural Language Processing*.

Yoshua Bengio, Rejean Ducharme, Pascal Vincent, and Christian Jauvin. 2003. A neural probabilistic language model. *JMLR*, 3(2):1137–1155.

Yoshua Bengio, Jérôme Louradour, Ronan Collobert, and Jason Weston. 2009. Curriculum learning. In *ICML*.

Nicola Bertoldi, Mauro Cettolo, Marcello Federico, and Christian Buck. 2012. Evaluating the Learning Curve of Domain Adaptive Statistical Machine-Translation Systems. In *Workshop on SMT*, pages 433–441, Montréal, Canada.

Mauro Cettolo, Nicola Bertoldi, Marcello Federico, Holger Schwenk, Loïc Barrault, and Christophe Servan. 2014. Translation project adaptation for MTenhanced computer assisted translation. *Machine Translation*, 28(2):127–150.

Kyunghyun Cho, Bart van Merriënboer, Caglar Gulcehre, Dzmitry Bahdanau, Fethi Bougares, Holger Schwenk, and Yoshua Bengio. 2014. Learning phrase representations using RNN encoder–decoder for statistical machine translation. In *EMNLP*, pages 1724–1734.

Kevin Duh, Graham Neubig, Katsuhito Sudoh, and Hajime Tsukada. 2013. Adaptation data selection using neural language models: Experiments in machine translation. In *ACL (2)*, pages 678–683.

George Foster and Roland Kuhn. 2007. Mixture-model adaptation for SMT. In *EMNLP*, pages 128–135.

Shahab Jalalvand. 2013. Improving language model adaptation using automatic data selection and neural network. In *RANLP*, pages 86–92.

Philipp Koehn and Josh Schroeder. 2007. Experiments in domain adaptation for statistical machine translation. In *Second Workshop on SMT*, pages 224–227, June.

Philipp Koehn, Franz Josef Och, and Daniel Marcu. 2003. Statistical phrase-based machine translation. In *HLT/NACL*, pages 127–133.

Philipp Koehn, Hieu Hoang, Alexandra Birch, Chris Callison-Burch, Marcello Federico, Nicola Bertoldi, Brooke Cowan, Wade Shen, Christine Moran, Richard Zens, Chris Dyer, Ondrej Bojar, Alexandra Constantin, and Evan Herbst. 2007. Moses: Open source toolkit for statistical machine translation. In *ACL, demonstration session.*

Stefan Kombrink, Tomas Mikolov, Martin Karafiát, and Lukás Burget. 2011. Recurrent neural network based language modeling in meeting recognition. In *INTERSPEECH*, pages 2877–2880.

Hai-Son Le, I. Oparin, A. Allauzen, J-L. Gauvain, and F. Yvon. 2011. Structured output layer neural network language model. In *ICASSP*, pages 5524–5527.

Hai-Son Le, Alexandre Allauzen, and François Yvon. 2012. Continuous space translation models with neural networks. In *NAACL*.

Tomáš Mikolov, Martin Karafiát, Lukáš Burget, Jan Černocký, and Sanjeev Khudanpur. 2010. Recurrent neural network based language model. In *Interspeech*, pages 1045–1048.

Tomáš Mikolov, A. Deoras, D. Povey, L. Burget, and J. Černocký. 2011. Strategies for training large scale neural network language models. In *ASRU*, pages 196–201.

Robert C. Moore and William Lewis. 2010. Intelligent selection of language model training data. In *ACL*, pages 220–224.

Franz Josef Och and Hermann Ney. 2003. A systematic comparison of various statistical alignement models. *Computational Linguistics*, 29(1):19–51.

Franz Josef Och. 2003. Minimum error rate training in statistical machine translation. In *ACL*, pages 160–167.

K. Papineni, S. Roukos, T. Ward, and W.J. Zhu. 2002. BLEU: a method for automatic evaluation of machine translation. In *ACL*, pages 311–318.

Junho Park, Xunying Liu, Mark J. F. Gales, and Phil C. Woodland. 2010. Improved neural network based language modelling and adaptation. In *Interspeech*, pages 1041–1044.

Holger Schwenk, Fethi Bougares, and Loïc Barrault. 2014. Efficient training strategies for deep neural network language models. In *NIPS workshop on Deep Learning and Representation Learning*.

Holger Schwenk. 2007. Continuous space language models. *Computer Speech and Language*, 21:492–518.

Holger Schwenk. 2012. Continuous space translation models for phrase-based statistical machine translation. In *Coling*, pages 1071–1080.

Holger Schwenk. 2013. CSLM - a modular open-source continuous space language modeling toolkit. In *Interspeech*, pages 1198–1202.

Yangyang Shia, Martha Larsona, and Catholijn M. Jonkera. 2014. Recurrent neural network language model adaptation with curriculum learning. *Computer Speech & Language*, 33(1):136–154.

Martin Sundermeyer, Ralf Schlüter, and Hermann Ney. 2012. LSTM neural networks for language modeling. In *Interspeech*.

I. Sutskever, O. Vinyals, and Q. Le. 2014. Sequence to sequence learning with neural networks. In *NIPS*, pages 3104–3112.

Jan Trmal, Jan Zelinka, and Ludek Müller. 2010. Adaptation of a feedforward articifical neural network using a linear transform. In *Text, Speech and Dialogue*, pages 423–430.

Kaisheng Yao, Dong Yu, Frank Seide, Hang Su, Li Deng, and Yifan Gong. 2012. Adaptation of context-dependent deep neural networks for automatic speech recognition. In *Spoken Language Technology Workshop (SLT), 2012 IEEE*, pages 366–369. IEEE.

Jason Yosinski, Jeff Clune, Yoshua Bengio, and Hod Lipson. 2014. How transferable are features in deep neural networks? In *NIPS*, pages 3320–3328.

Observed versus latent features for knowledge base and text inference

Kristina Toutanova
Microsoft Research
Redmond, WA, USA

Danqi Chen*
Computer Science Department
Stanford University

Abstract

In this paper we show the surprising effectiveness of a simple observed features model in comparison to latent feature models on two benchmark knowledge base completion datasets, FB15K and WN18. We also compare latent and observed feature models on a more challenging dataset derived from FB15K, and additionally coupled with textual mentions from a web-scale corpus. We show that the observed features model is most effective at capturing the information present for entity pairs with textual relations, and a combination of the two combines the strengths of both model types.

1 Introduction

Representing information about real-world entities and their relations in structured knowledge bases (KBs) enables numerous applications. Large, collaboratively created knowledge bases have become recently available (some examples are Freebase (Bollacker et al., 2008), YAGO (Suchanek et al., 2007), and DBPedia (Auer et al., 2007)), but even though they are impressively large, their coverage is far from complete. This has motivated research in automatically deriving new facts to extend a manually built knowledge base, by using information from the existing knowledge base and information from textual mentions of entities in documents.

Many statistical models for predicting new links in knowledge bases have been applied to this task, with most successful ones being latent feature models that learn continuous representations for entities and relations (Bordes et al., 2011; Nickel et al., 2011; Bordes et al., 2013), and observed feature models which predict based on observable features in the knowledge graphs (Lao et al., 2011; Riedel et al., 2013). Additionally, studies have looked at the contribution of text-based extraction to knowledge base completion (Lao et al., 2012; Gardner et al., 2013).

In this paper we compare empirically a very simple observed features model to state-of-the-art latent feature models recently applied to two commonly used datasets for knowledge base completion: a dataset adapted from the Freebase KB, called FB15K (Bordes et al., 2013) and a dataset derived from the WordNet graph WN18, also introduced in (Bordes et al., 2013). We show that the simple observed features model substantially outperforms latent feature models, possibly due to the arguably unrealistic redundancy in the KB graphs of these datasets. Nevertheless, it is intriguing that the latent feature models studied are not able to learn the target concept as well, even given a large number of latent features.

We also construct a harder, perhaps more realistic dataset derived from FB15K, in which we remove near-duplicate or inverse-duplicate relations. We show that in this new dataset our studied latent feature models substantially outperform the observed feature models. When we augment the newly constructed dataset with textual mentions derived from the ClueWeb 12 web-scale document collection, we see that the observed features model is more powerful than the latent feature models, but also that a combination of the two is superior to either of them.

2 Related Work

There has been a large amount of work on statistical models for knowledge base completion. Nickel et al. (2015) provide a recent overview.

Most related to our current focus is recent work applying latent feature models to the FB15K and WN18 datasets (Bordes et al., 2013; Wang et al., 2014; Yang et al., 2015), work containing comparisons between observed and latent feature mod-

* Parts of this research were conducted during the author's internship at Microsoft Research.

Proceedings of the 3rd Workshop on Continuous Vector Space Models and their Compositionality (CVSC), pages 57–66,
Beijing, China, July 26-31, 2015.

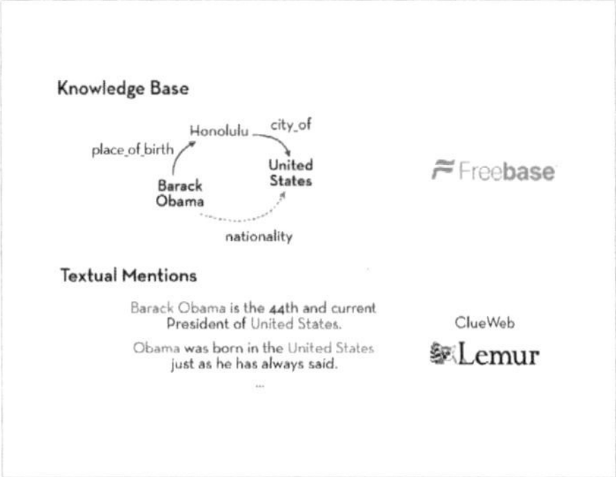

Figure 1: A knowledge base fragment coupled with textual mentions of pairs of entities.

els (Dong et al., 2014; Nickel et al., 2014), and work using inference from both text and knowledge base relations (Lao et al., 2012; Riedel et al., 2013; Dong et al., 2014; Gardner et al., 2014).

Our work differs from this prior work in that we compare a very simple form of observed feature models, based on using only direct links between candidate entity pairs, to state-of-the-art latent feature models on two benchmark datasets, with surprising results.

Our work on using textual mentions for knowledge base inference differs from prior work in the scale and richness of the knowledge base and textual relations used, as well as in that we evaluate the impact of text not only on mentioned entity pairs like (Gardner et al., 2014; Riedel et al., 2013) but on all links. We represent knowledge base and textual patterns in a single knowledge graph, like Lao et al. (2012) and Riedel et al. (2013), but refine the learning method to treat textual relations differently in the loss function, to maximize predictive performance on the knowledge base relations. We show the impact of observed and latent feature models and their combination in knowledge graphs with and without textual relations.

3 Models for knowledge base completion

We begin by introducing notation to define the task, largely following the terminology in Nickel et al. (2015). We assume knowledge bases are represented using RDF triples, in the form (*subject, predicate, object*), where the subject and object are entities and the predicate is the type of relation. For example, the KB fragment shown in Figure 1 is shown as a knowledge graph, where the entities are the nodes, and the relations are shown as directed labeled edges: we see three entities which participate in three relation instances indicated by the edges.

The task we are interested in is, given a training KB consisting of entities with some relations between them, to predict new relations (links) that do not appear in the training KB. For example, the triple (*Barack Obama, nationality, United States*) could be predicted from the training KB triples (*Barack Obama, place_of_birth, Honolulu*) and (*Honolulu, city_of, United States*). More specifically, we will build models that rank candidate entities for given queries $(e_1, r, ?)$ or $(?, r, e_2)$, which ask about the subject or object of a given relation.

The following notation will help us define the statistical models over knowledge graphs that we consider. Let $\mathcal{E} = (e_1, e_2, \ldots, e_{N_e})$ denote the set of entities in the knowledge graph and let $\mathcal{R} = (r_1, r_2, \ldots, r_{N_r})$ denote the set of relation types. We denote each possible triple as $x_{i,j,k} = (e_i, r_k, e_j)$ and model its presence with a binary random variable $y_{i,j,k} \in \{0, 1\}$ which indicates whether the triple exists. We will focus on models that score possible triples $x_{i,j,k}$ using either *observed features* from the knowledge graph or *latent features* of the three elements of the triple. Both model classes use scoring functions $f(x_{i,j,k}; \Theta)$ that represent the model's confidence in the existence of the triple. We first specify the forms of scoring functions we consider in this study, and later detail the loss functions used for training model parameters. We use the same loss function (as a function of triple scores) for training all models in this study.

3.1 Observed feature models

We consider an extremely simple form of observed feature models, which can be seen as an impoverished variant of path ranking (PRA) for KB completion (Lao and Cohen, 2010; Lao et al., 2011). In particular we define features for existing paths of length one for candidate triples (e_i, r_k, e_j). These can be paths from e_i to e_j or from e_j to e_i. Length one paths from e_i to e_j: we define binary features of the form $\mathbf{1}(r'\&r_k)$, which fire when the triple e_i, r', e_j exists in the training knowledge graph, and $r' \neq r_k$. This feature type captures correlations among multiple relation types for the same entity pair – for example, if someone lives in a certain city, they might be likely to work in the same city. Length one paths from e_j to e_i: we define binary indicator features of the form $\mathbf{1}(r'_{inv} \& r_k)$, which fire when the triple e_j, r', e_i exists in the training knowledge graph. Here r' can capture the correlation with inverse relations, for example *nationality* and *people_of_nationality*.

Such features will fire only if the candidate entity pair (e_i, e_j) is already directly connected in the training knowledge graph (by a link in either direction). Thus such features are expected to be helpful only when there are multiple correlated relation types that tend to connect similar sets of entity pairs. In the experiments section, we will show that this is indeed the case for two commonly used KB completion datasets we study. It is also true for knowledge graphs augmented with textual links, where each co-occurrence of (e_i, e_j) in a document collection induces a link of a textually-defined relation type. In addition to the features looking at length one paths, for the observed feature models we define an indicator feature for every entity and relation in the triple. This captures a bias for these entities to occur in the subject or object position of the relation. The features are $\mathbf{1}(e_i = s \& r_k)$ and $\mathbf{1}(e_j = o \& r_k)$, where s and o indicate the subject and object positions, respectively. These features can capture the frequency with which each argument of the relation is occupied by a specific entity. For example, we can learn that *United States* is a common nationality for entities in Freebase.

Given a feature vector $\Phi_{i,j,k}$, the score of a triple is defined by its dot product with a parameter vector, which contains a weight for each feature: $f(x_{i,j,k}; \Theta) = \Phi_{i,j,k}^T \Theta$.

3.2 Latent feature models

In latent feature models, the score of a candidate triple is assumed to depend only on learned latent features of the entities and relations, and possibly additional global parameters. In this work we consider two simple latent feature models, which have been found to be competitive or outperform more complex alternatives in prior work (Yang et al., 2015; Riedel et al., 2013).

The first model we consider is model E (abbreviated from ENTITY), which captures the compatibility between entities and the subject and object positions of relations. It can be seen as learning a soft notion of entity types. The model was applied to knowledge-base completion for text-augmented

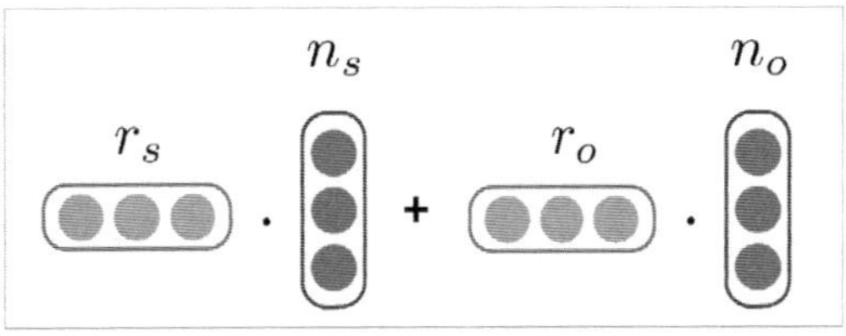

Figure 2: The continuous representations for model E.

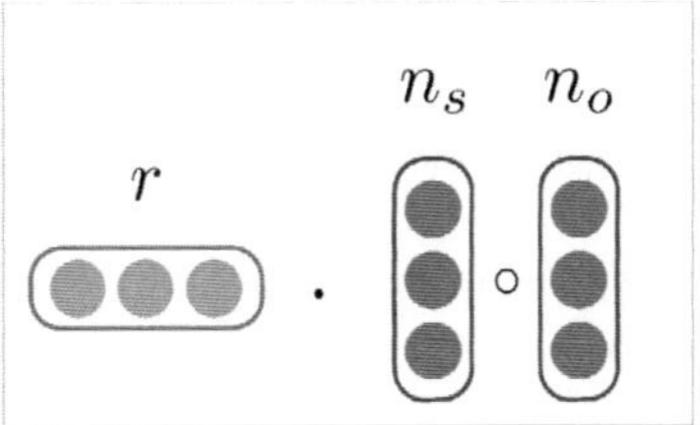

Figure 3: The continuous representations for model DISTMULT.

knowledge graphs using a universal schema approach (Riedel et al., 2013). For each relation type, the model learns two latent feature vectors r_s and r_o of some dimensionality K. For each entity (node) e_i, the model also learns a latent feature vector n_i of the same dimensionality. The model is depicted in Figure 2. The score of a candidate triple (e_s, r, e_o) where the sub-scripts s and o are used to indicate subject and object positions, respectively, is defined as: $f(x_{s,r,o}) = {r_s}^T n_s + {r_o}^T n_o$.

The second model, DISTMULT, is a special form of a bilinear model like RESCAL (Nickel et al., 2011), where the non-diagonal entries in the relation matrices are assumed to be zero. This model was proposed in Yang et al. (2015) under the name DISTMULT, and was shown to outperform the more highly parameterized bilinear model, as well as the additive model TRANSE (Bordes et al., 2013). In this model, each entity e_i is assigned a latent feature vector (embedding) n_i of dimensionality K and each relation type is assigned an embedding r of the same dimensionality. The model form is shown in Figure 3. The score of a candidate triple (e_s, r, e_o) is defined as: $f(x_{s,r,o}) = r^T (n_s \circ n_o)$.

If there are N_e entities, N_r relations, and latent feature vectors of dimensionality K are used, model E has $KN_e + 2KN_r$ parameters and model DISTMULT has $KN_e + KN_r$ parameters.

Combined models

We also consider weighted combinations of latent feature models and observed feature models in a method similar to the one used in the Additive Relational Effects Model of Nickel et al. (2014). Given scoring functions $f_1(x_{i,j,j}, \Theta_1)$ and $f_2(x_{i,j,j}, \Theta_2)$ defined by two different models, we define a combined model for which the score of a triple is a weighted combination of the scores by the two models $w_1 f_1(x_{i,j,j}, \Theta_1) + w_2 f_2(x_{i,j,j}, \Theta_2)$. The component models could be latent of observed feature models, and the combination weights are either uniform (set to 1), or non-uniform and selected via a grid search on a validation set. We train the parameters of combined models jointly, by minimizing the loss function based on the combined scores.

3.3 Training loss function

Our loss function is motivated by the link prediction task and the performance measures used to assess model performance. As mentioned earlier, the task is to predict the subject or object entity for given held-out triples (e_1, r, e_2), i.e. to rank all entities with respect to their likelihood of filling the respective position in the triple. We would thus like the model to score correct triples (e_1, r, e_2) higher than incorrect triples (e', r, e_2) and (e_1, r, e') which differ from the correct triple by one entity. One could use a margin-based loss function as used in several approaches (Nickel et al., 2015). We use an approximation to the negative log-likelihood of the correct entity filler. We define the conditional probabilities $p(e_2|e_1, r)$ and $p(e_1|r, e_2)$ for object and subject entities given the relation and the other argument as follows: $p(e_2|e_1, r_k; \Theta) = \frac{e^{f(x_{e_1,e_2,k};\Theta)}}{\sum_{e'_2 \in Neg(e_1,r_k,?)} e^{f(x_{e_1,e'_2,k};\Theta)}}$.

Here the denominator is defined using a set of entities that do not fill the object position in any relation triple $(e_1, r, ?)$ in the training knowledge graph. Since the number of such entities is impractically large, we sample negative triples from the full set (we use 200 negative examples in our experiments). In some settings we also limit the candidate entities to ones that have types consistent with the position in the relation triple (Chang et al., 2014; Yang et al., 2015). We derive approximate type information automatically (as discussed below), but such information could also be present in the knowledge graphs.

Conditional probabilities for subject entities given relation and object are defined analogously, as follows: $p(e_1|r_k, e_2; \Theta) = \frac{e^{f(x_{e_1,e_2,k};\Theta)}}{\sum_{e'_1 \in Neg(?,r_k,e_2)} e^{f(x_{e'_1,e_2,k};\Theta)}}$

Given the definition of subject and object conditional probabilities for triples, our training loss function is defined as the sum of the negative log-probabilities of observed triples, also including an L2 penalty on the model parameters. If X denotes the set of all triples in the training knowledge graph, the training loss is defined as:

$$\begin{aligned} L(X, \Theta, \lambda) &= - \sum_{x_{e_1,e_2,r_k} \in X} \log p(e_2|e_1, r_k; \Theta) \\ &\quad - \sum_{x_{e_1,e_2,r_k} \in X} \log p(e_1|r_k, e_2; \Theta) \\ &\quad + \lambda \Theta^T \Theta \end{aligned}$$

3.3.1 Entity types

We define the type of an entity e as a pair of sets of relation types $[R^s, R^o]$; R^s is the set of relation types r for which e is the source node of a link with type r in the training knowledge graph and R^o is the set of relation types for which e is the target node of link with type r. For each relation, we compute a set of allowable entity types by checking the percentage of its arguments that have a given type and restricting the allowable types to the top t (chosen on a validation set, usually two or three). For example, for the subject position of a *parents* relation the most frequent type would be $parent^s$ (meaning subject of *parent*). A second frequent type might be $born\_in^s$ meaning subject of *born_in*. Using this construction we define the compatibility between entities and relation argument positions, which prunes the space of candidates quite significantly in many cases, while still maintaining a high upper bound on achievable performance. Details on the impact of usage of types are presented in Section 4.

3.4 Representation and loss for text-augmented knowledge graphs

In addition to knowledge graphs containing only relations r from a given manually developed ontology, we consider knowledge graphs augmented with textual relations derived from sentence co-occurrences of entity pairs. This follows the approaches of Lao et al. (2012) anf Riedel et al. (2013), who represent both textual and knowledge base relations in a single graph of "universal" relations, which allows joint reasoning from

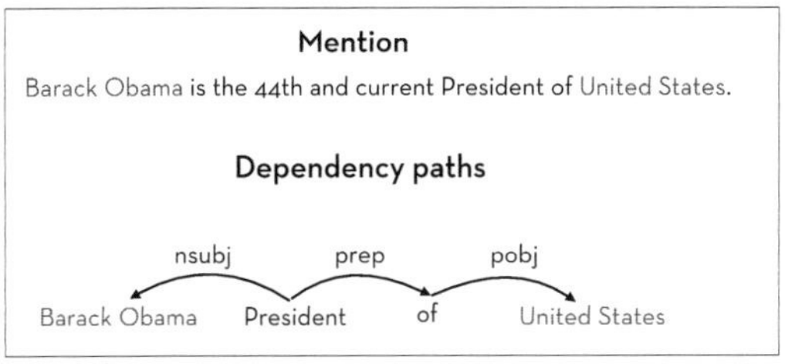

Figure 4: Textual relation extracted from an entity pair mention.

the two types of relations. Figure 4 shows the lexicalized dependency path between two entities that occur together in a sentence. An instance of textual relation of type "$\xleftarrow{\text{nsubj}}$ *president* $\xrightarrow{\text{prep}}$ *of* $\xrightarrow{\text{obj}}$ *United States*", corresponding to the sentence is added to the knowledge graph based on this occurrence. Textual co-occurrences of entity pairs often express relations between the entities, which might correspond exactly or approximately to knowledge base relations. Text could thus be a strong signal for predicting knowledge base relations (Lao et al., 2012).

Once a knowledge graph is augmented with textual relations, we can train the same models as before, treating knowledge base and text relations in a uniform manner. However, since we are only interested in predicting knowledge-base relations, it might be suboptimal for the model to try to fit its parameters toward predicting textual relations as hard as it tries to optimize for knowledge base relations. In other words, the part of the loss function looking at subject and object probabilities for textual relations t is only useful to provide an auxiliary prediction task which is beneficial for the main task using a multi-task learning setting. Therefore, one might choose an optimal weight τ which could be expected to be less than the weight of the primary loss function. We thus consider a modified loss function for KB+text model training, defined as follows. If the set of all triples using KB relations is X and the set of all triples using text relations is T, the loss is defined as $L(X \cup T, \Theta) = L(X, \Theta) + \tau L(T, \Theta)$. In the experiments section we will see that this simple modification can provide large performance benefits.

4 Experiments

We perform experiments with latent and observed feature models and their combination. We first present results on the FB15K dataset, which was originality constructed (using Freebase) by Bordes et al. (2013) and was subsequently used in several research studies (Wang et al., 2014; Yang et al., 2015). The number of relations and triples in the training, development and test portions of the datasets are given in Table 5.

4.1 Task and Evaluation Protocol

Given a set of triples in a set disjoint from a training knowledge graph, we test models on predicting the subject or object of each triple, given the relation type and the other argument. We rank all entities in the training knowledge base in order of their likelihood of filling the argument position. We report the mean reciprocal rank of the correct entity, as well as HITS@10 – the percent of test triples for which the correct argument was ranked in the top ten. We use *filtered* measures following the protocol proposed in Bordes et al. (2013) – that is, when we rank entities for a given position, we remove all other entities that are known to be part of an existing triple in the training, development, or test set. This avoids penalizing the model for ranking other correct fillers higher than the tested argument. We thus report filtered mean reciprocal rank (labeled MRR in the Figures), and filtered HITS@10. In the figures we present MRR values scaled by 100, so that the maximum possible MRR is 100.

Implementation details and hyper-parameter settings

For all models implemented in this work, we trained the models using the loss function presented in Section 3.3, using $\lambda = 1$ as the weight of the $L2$ regularizer. We used a batch learning parameter optimization method, after initial experiments showed it did better than stochastic optimization using AdaGrad. We experimented with LBFGS (Liu and Nocedal, 1989) and RProp (Riedmiller and Braun, 1993), and found RProp to converge faster to similar values of the objective for the latent feature models. All reported results use RProp. We also used early stopping to terminate optimization when the MRR on the validation set stopped improving.

We chose the optimal number of latent features via a grid search to optimize MRR on the validation set, testing the values 10,50,100,200,500,and 1,000. Similarly, we performed a grid search over the values of the parameter τ which weighs

Dataset	Relations	Entities	Triples in Train / Validation / Test			% Test Linked
FB15K	1,345	14,951	483,142	50,000	59,071	80.9
FB15KSelected	237	14,541	272,115	17,535	20,466	0
WN18	18	40,943	141,442	5,000	5,000	94.0

Figure 5: Datasets used in this study. FB15K and WN18 have been used in prior work and FB15KSelected is a new dataset derived from FB15K and ClueWeb (described in text).

Model	FB15K Type Constraints		FB15K No Type Constraints	
	MRR	HITS@10	MRR	HITS@10
E	22.7	34.0	21.8	33.6
DISTMULT	63.1	79.0	55.5	79.7
E+DISTMULT	65.9	81.0	56.2	78.3
TransE			32.0	53.9
DISTMULT (Yang et al., 2015)			36.0	57.7
TransH (bern.) (Wang et al., 2014)				64.4
NodeFeat	21.7	32.6	21.6	32.4
LinkFeat	79.1	80.8	77.9	80.4
Node+LinkFeat	**82.1**	**86.1**	82.2	87.0

Figure 6: Results on FB15K with and without type constraints for candidate filtering in training and testing.

the textual relations loss, testing values in the set $\{0.01, 0.1, 0.25, 0.5, 1\}$.

4.2 Experiments on KB Completion using FB15K and WN18

We present experiments of different models introduced in this paper on these datasets, and additionally include results reported in prior work. We also evaluate the impact of our use of types as hard constraints in training and testing, and how these constraints impact latent feature models versus observed feature models.

Figure 6 presents the results under two settings: using automatically derived types versus not using them. The results not using types are presented in the right half of the Figure. The first six rows report performance measures obtained using latent feature models. The first three models presented are the ones defined in Section 3.2 and implemented in this work. We evaluate these models when type constraints are used or when they are not used. The next three rows report results from prior work by directly copying reported numbers from the respective papers. Since these papers did not use type constraints, we list the results in the right two columns only. The model TransE was proposed in (Bordes et al., 2013) but we use the results from the implementation of (Yang et al., 2015), because these results were higher. The TransH (bern.) results are obtained by the model presented in (Wang et al., 2014).

The last three rows show results from observed feature models, as defined in Section 3.1, where the first model uses only node features, the second uses only direct link features, and the third uses both feature types.

The type constraints were defined using the method presented in Section 3.3.1. We choose the best settings for the method based on coverage of the correct triples in the validation set. Given the hard pruning of candidates by type filtering, the method using types has less than 100 percent achievable accuracy — the oracle HITS@10 by using type constraints is 98.3. We found that the number of latent features did not have a large impact on performance for model E, but did have large impact for the other two models. Using 500 hidden dimensions was optimal for these two models. Even though the form of the scoring function for DISTMULT is exactly the same as defined in (Yang et al., 2015), we obtain much higher performance. We attribute this to the larger number of hidden dimensions (500 vs 100), and the use of the softmax-based loss function with 200 negative examples and batch training.[1] As seen, the impact of the type constraints is large and positive, especially on the MRR values. Our implementation of these embedding models outperforms the other recent results by TransH (Wang et al., 2014), which we also attribute to the loss function and optimization.

The most striking result on this dataset is seen in the last two rows of the Table, where we can

[1]We chose the optimal number of hidden dimensions to optimize MRR on the development set. We found that performance improved with dimensionality up to 500 dimensions. For DISTMULT with type constraints, the MRR for dimensionality $\{10, 100, 500\}$ was $\{35.2, 55.8, 63.1\}$, respectively.

Model	FB15KSelected					
	MRR a/t/nt			HITS@10 a/t/nt		
	Without Text					
E	23.5	20.2	24.4	35.6	31.7	36.9
DISTMULT	25.3	20.9	26.7	40.8	34.8	42.6
E+DISTMULT	26.6	23.1	27.7	43.0	38.4	44.4
NodeFeat	23.5	20.3	24.5	35.6	31.7	36.8
LinkFeat	6.3	3.1	7.3	7.9	5.2	8.7
Node+LinkFeat	22.6	19.3	23.7	34.7	30.6	36.0
Combined	26.8	23.1	28.0	42.8	37.8	44.3
	With Text					
E+DISTMULT ($\tau = 1$)	26.6	24.0	27.3	41.3	38.4	42.2
E+DISTMULT ($\tau = .1$)	27.4	24.3	**28.3**	43.8	39.8	**45.0**
Node+LinkFeat	27.2	**39.6**	23.4	41.4	**60.5**	35.5
Combined (($\tau = .1$)	**29.3**	**39.1**	26.3	**46.2**	**60.0**	41.9

Figure 7: Results on FB15KSelected with and without addition of textual links. Model Combined is a combination of the latent feature models E and DISTMULT and the observed feature model Node+LinkFeat.

Model	WN18	
	MRR	HITS@10
TRANSE (Bordes et al., 2013)		89.2
DISTMULT (Yang et al., 2015)	83.0	94.2
BILNEAR (Yang et al., 2015)	89.0	92.8
TransH (unif) (Wang et al., 2014)		86.7
NodeFeat	2.9	5.0
LinkFeat	93.8	93.9
Node+LinkFeat	94.0	94.3

Figure 8: Results on WN18 using performance reported in prior work as well as performance of observed feature models.

see the performance of the observed feature models based on direct links. The performance of these models (in MRR) is much higher that the performance of the latent feature models obtained in this work and in prior work. This is perhaps not so surprising when we look at the number of test set triples (e_1, r, e_2) for which either (e_1, r', e_2) or (e_2, r', e_1) occur in the training set – i.e., which are directly linked in the training knowledge graph. This number is almost 81% (reported in Table 5), and explains why the observed features model which uses this information directly can do so well. What is more surprising is that latent feature models have not approached this performance, even given a large number of latent feature dimensions. We see this is an interesting datapoint which can motivate analysis and improvement in the state-of-the-art in knowledge base completion using latent variable models.

Two other interesting results from these experiments are that the observed feature model using only entity features (NodeFeat) has almost the same performance as the latent feature model E and both can be seen as learning a unigram distribution over entities for argument positions of relations. Additionally, the observed feature models are not substantially affected by the use of type constraints, since they effectively learn to model similar type concepts using the features.

We also tested the models on WN18, and report results from prior work using latent feature models as well as our implementation of the observed feature models in Figure 8. As seen, the observed feature models using link features strongly outperform prior work in the MRR measure (achieving around 45% error reduction over the best previously reported results), and are comparable to the best models according to the HITS@10 measure. As shown in Table 5, 94.0 of test triple entities are directly linked in the training KB, explaining the success of these simple models.

Given our analysis of the FB15k and WN18 datasets and the power of a simple observed features model, we are motivated to construct a more realistic knowledge base completion dataset for which we can assume that trivially entailed facts (due to relation symmetry or the presence of inverse relations) have already been inferred and the task is to entail facts requiring non-trivial inference. To this effect we construct a subset of FB15K, which we term FB15KSelected, and which represents a more challenging learning setting.

4.3 Experiments using knowledge graph and text inference on FB15KSelected

The dataset FB15KSelected[2] was constructed by first limiting the set of relations in FB15K to the most frequently used 401 relations (a setting using this subset of frequent relations was also used in (Yang et al., 2015)). We then automatically detected near-duplicate and inverse relations by checking whether the set of entity pairs in the relations is either almost the same (at least 97% of the pairs are in the intersection), or whether the set of inverse entity pairs is almost the same e.g. comparing $[e_1, e_2]$ for r to the set $[e_2, e_1]$ for r'. For example, this process detected that the relation */award/award_nominee* is inverse of */award_nominee/award*. Given this information, we filtered the set of relations to keep only one of a set of inverse or duplicate relations; this resulted in 237 relations, and we limited the training, validation, and development set triples to these relations. We also filtered from the validation and test sets any triples whose entity pairs were directly linked in the training database. Such direct links could admittedly be legitimately present in a realistic scenario but we excluded them to avoid additional trivial cases which could have not been detected via the prior filtering step. The statistics for this resulting dataset are shown in Table 5.

While for this more realistic dataset we have excluded all direct KB links for test entity pairs, there is a realistic source of direct relations between test entity pairs – textual relations expressed by sentences containing these pairs of entities. We use the ClueWeb12 [3] corpus coupled with Freebase mention annotations (Gabrilovich et al., 2013) to extract textual relations for all entity pairs in the knowledge base. We extract textual patterns from 200 million dependency-parsed sentences and we represent the textual relations via the fully lexicalized dependency path connecting two entities, as shown in Figure 4. After pruning, we use 25,000 unique textual relations and add links to the training knowledge graph based on these relations. There are 6.6 million links induced from the textual relations for the FB15KSelected knowledge base. Of the test KB triples, 23.3% of the entity pairs have textual mentions. For the training set, 31% of the entity pairs that have a KB link have a textual mention, and having a mention increases the chance that a random entity pair has a relation from .1% to 4.2% – a forty-fold increase.

Figure 7 shows the results for this dataset – the upper portion contains results for models not using textual mentions, and the lower part contains results of models also using the text. The results are shown using the MRR and HITS@10 measures, and these are further broken down into overall/with textual mentions/without textual mentions (a/t/nt).

For the setting where no textual mentions are used, we see that the latent feature models outperform the observed feature models (since there are no direct links in the training set for test triples, the observed features model LinkFeat has performance which is random subject to the type constraints (and where ties are broken by order of appearance in the training set)). Using node features only is best for the observed feature models, and the overall MRR of this model (23.5), is substantially below that of the best latent feature model, E+DISTMULT with overall MRR of 26.6. A model which combines the latent and observed features (shown in row 7), does not bring substantial improvement.

The second (lower) part of the Figure shows model results when the training knowledge graph is expanded with textual relations. First, for the best latent feature model E+DISTMULT which treats knowledge base and textual relations uniformly, using $\tau = 1$ as in the universal schema approach (Riedel et al., 2013), we see no improvement from using the textual mentions. Indeed, there is an improvement in MRR on the test triples that have mentions (23.1 to 24.0), but performance degrades on the more numerous test cases without mentions. When τ is optimized via grid search to a value of $\tau = .1$ we see a good improvement to overall MRR 27.4 due to using text, which holds for cases with mentions as well as ones without mentions. The observed features model benefits from text strongly, and in particular the MRR on test triples with mentions increases from 19.3 to 39.6. The performance on triples without mentions is very low, however. Since the latent and observed feature models have complementary strengths, their combination (last row in the Figure) substantially outperforms both kinds of models, reaching an overall MRR of 29.3 and overall

[2] A release of the dataset will be available soon. Contact the authors for more details if interested.

[3] http://www.lemurproject.org/clueweb12.php/

HITS@10 of 46.2. The MRR on test triples with mentions is almost doubled compared to the models not using text.

Conclusion

This work provided two main lessons for knowledge base completion. First, we showed that the presence of relations between candidate pairs can be an extremely strong signal in some cases, and that this signal was not effectively captured by the studied latent feature models. Second, we showed that textual links extracted from a large document collection and added to an existing KB-completion dataset brought substantial improvements, especially on test cases with textual occurrences. It was beneficial to use the direct textual links as features in an observed features model and to combine that with a latent feature model, to effectively capture inferences among KB relations and direct cues from text. We also showed that in a dataset where training and test triples are not artificially limited to only ones that have textual mentions, it becomes important to tradeoff the weight of the loss incurred from textual versus KB relations.

Acknowledgements

We would like to thank Jianfeng Gao, Scott Yih, Patrick Pantel, Michael Gamon, Hoifung Poon and the anonymous reviewers for useful suggestions.

References

Sören Auer, Christian Bizer, Georgi Kobilarov, Jens Lehmann, Richard Cyganiak, and Zachary Ives. 2007. *Dbpedia: A nucleus for a web of open data*. Springer.

Kurt Bollacker, Colin Evans, Praveen Paritosh, Tim Sturge, and Jamie Taylor. 2008. Freebase: a collaboratively created graph database for structuring human knowledge. In *Proceedings of the 2008 ACM SIGMOD international conference on Management of data*, pages 1247–1250. ACM.

Antoine Bordes, Jason Weston, Ronan Collobert, and Yoshua Bengio. 2011. Learning structured embeddings of knowledge bases. In *Conference on Artificial Intelligence*, number EPFL-CONF-192344.

Antoine Bordes, Nicolas Usunier, Alberto Garcia-Duran, Jason Weston, and Oksana Yakhnenko. 2013. Translating embeddings for modeling multi-relational data. In *Advances in Neural Information Processing Systems (NIPS)*.

Kai-Wei Chang, Wen-tau Yih, Bishan Yang, and Christopher Meek. 2014. Typed tensor decomposition of knowledge bases for relation extraction. In *Empirical Methods in Natural Language Processing (EMNLP)*.

Xin Dong, Evgeniy Gabrilovich, Geremy Heitz, Wilko Horn, Ni Lao, Kevin Murphy, Thomas Strohmann, Shaohua Sun, and Wei Zhang. 2014. Knowledge vault: A web-scale approach to probabilistic knowledge fusion. In *International Conference on Knowledge Discovery and Data Mining (KDD)*.

Evgeniy Gabrilovich, Michael Ringgaard, and Amarnag Subramanya. 2013. FACC1: Freebase annotation of ClueWeb corpora, Version 1 (release date 2013-06-26, format version 1, correction level 0).

Matt Gardner, Partha Pratim Talukdar, Bryan Kisiel, and Tom Mitchell. 2013. Improving learning and inference in a large knowledge-base using latent syntactic cues. In *Empirical Methods in Natural Language Processing (EMNLP)*.

Matt Gardner, Partha Talukdar, Jayant Krishnamurthy, and Tom Mitchell. 2014. Incorporating vector space similarity in random walk inference over knowledge bases. In *Empirical Methods in Natural Language Processing (EMNLP)*.

Ni Lao and William W Cohen. 2010. Relational retrieval using a combination of path-constrained random walks. *Machine learning*.

Ni Lao, Tom Mitchell, and William W Cohen. 2011. Random walk inference and learning in a large scale knowledge base. In *Empirical Methods in Natural Language Processing (EMNLP)*.

Ni Lao, Amarnag Subramanya, Fernando Pereira, and William W Cohen. 2012. Reading the web with learned syntactic-semantic inference rules. In *Empirical Methods in Natural Language Processing and Computational Natural Language Learning (EMNLP/CoNLL)*.

Dong C Liu and Jorge Nocedal. 1989. On the limited memory bfgs method for large scale optimization. *Mathematical programming*, 45(1-3):503–528.

Maximilian Nickel, Volker Tresp, and Hans-Peter Kriegel. 2011. A three-way model for collective learning on multi-relational data. In *Proceedings of the 28th international conference on machine learning (ICML-11)*, pages 809–816.

Maximilian Nickel, Xueyan Jiang, and Volker Tresp. 2014. Reducing the rank in relational factorization models by including observable patterns. In Z. Ghahramani, M. Welling, C. Cortes, N.D. Lawrence, and K.Q. Weinberger, editors, *Advances in Neural Information Processing Systems 27*, pages 1179–1187. Curran Associates, Inc.

Maximilian Nickel, Kevin Murphy, Volker Tresp, and Evgeniy Gabrilovich. 2015. A review of relational machine learning for knowledge graphs: From multi-relational link prediction to automated knowledge graph construction. *arXiv preprint arXiv:1503.00759*.

Sebastian Riedel, Limin Yao, Benjamin M. Marlin, and Andrew McCallum. 2013. Relation extraction with matrix factorization and universal schemas. In *North American Chapter of the Association for Computational Linguistics: Human Language Technologies (NAACL-HLT)*.

Martin Riedmiller and Heinrich Braun. 1993. A direct adaptive method for faster backpropagation learning: The rprop algorithm. In *Neural Networks, 1993., IEEE International Conference on*, pages 586–591. IEEE.

Fabian M Suchanek, Gjergji Kasneci, and Gerhard Weikum. 2007. Yago: a core of semantic knowledge. In *Proceedings of the 16th international conference on World Wide Web*, pages 697–706. ACM.

Zhen Wang, Jianwen Zhang, Jianlin Feng, and Zheng Chen. 2014. Knowledge graph embedding by translating on hyperplanes. In *Proceedings of the Twenty-Eighth AAAI Conference on Artificial Intelligence*, pages 1112–1119.

Bishan Yang, Wen-tau Yih, Xiaodong He, Jianfeng Gao, and Li Deng. 2015. Embedding entities and relations for learning and inference in knowledge bases. In *International Conference on Learning Representations (ICLR)*.

Author Index